# the power of contemporary architecture

edited by peter cook and neil spiller

ACADEMY EDITIONS

the po

wer of

We would like to thank Laura Allen, without
whom this book would not have happened

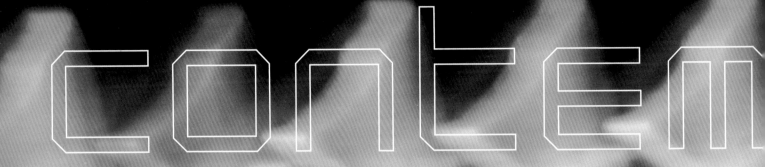

First published in Great Britain in 1999 by
ACADEMY EDITIONS

a division of
JOHN WILEY & SONS
Baffins Lane
Chichester
West Sussex PO19 1UD

ISBN 0-471-98419-1

Other Wiley Editorial Offices
New York • Weinheim • Brisbane • Singapore • Toronto

Design: Christian Küsters, Design Assistance: Peter Butler
Photography (Cover Sequence): Paul Wesley Griggs

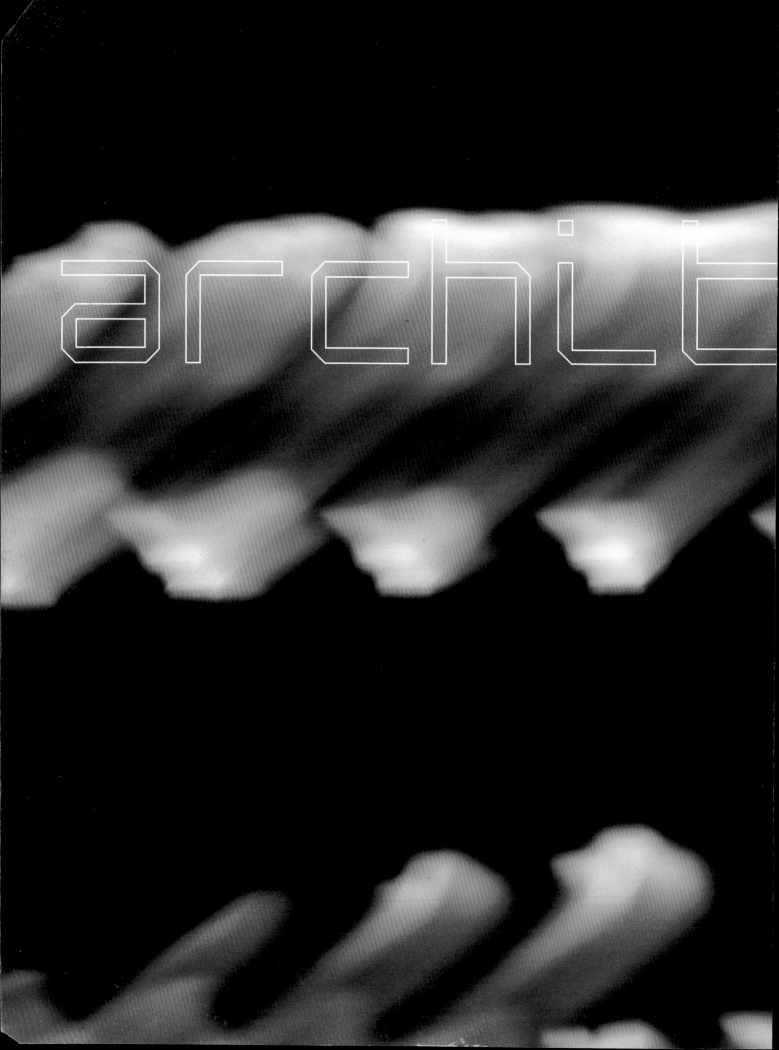

## foreword

### Brian Clarke

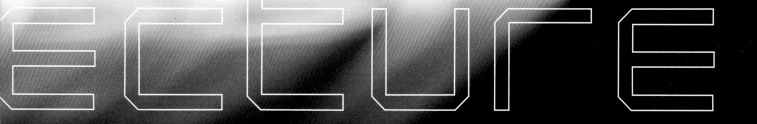

Many artists shy away from discussion of their work like the plague. Architects are different. The multiplicity of disciplines and skills involved in the creation of a building demands the continuous exchange of ideas and practice. On the whole, architects enjoy talking, and in general, architectural students like to listen to them. (You only have to compare lecture attendances in art schools to those in architecture departments to see the truth of this).

In the jungle of modern, cut-price education, the lecture programme of visiting architects is usually the first 'luxury' to bite the dust. Yet, it is this very exchange and interaction between practising architect and student that provides the oxygen for progress, development and change. Nothing has more profound an impact on the creative process than exposure to radical thinking and conflicting philosophies.

The vastly different ways in which designers approach and solve problems are often as exciting and informative as the problems themselves. Poetry harnessed to practice is a phenomenon that can be expressed in a huge diversity of ways. Only by direct access to that variety through contact with a large number of experimental architects can students hope to acquire a clear picture of their medium's potential.

In this context, men like Frank Lowe, the creative force behind a huge empire that spans forty countries, are pivotal. Having played a central role in the forming of the creative advertising industry and at various times boasting such celebrated figures as Alan Parker, Ridley Scott, David Puttnam and David Bailey on his team, Frank Lowe was unquestionably one of the key people to drag advertising out of the doldrums of post-war misery and into the hot-bed of creative energy that it is today.

Lowe has an enduring respect for excellence and discovery and believes absolutely in the importance of design in society. But more importantly, he turns this respect into practical help by funding, once again, our lecture programme at the Bartlett School of Architecture, University College, London. Without his direct support, we would be lamentably deprived of one of the most exciting and complex lecture programmes anywhere in the world today.

The creative double act of Frank Lowe and Peter Cook is a winning formula and I know I speak for all of us who are involved in the Bartlett when I acknowledge our debt and thanks to them both, but especially to our new friend Frank Lowe who has made it possible.

# Introduction

Peter Cook

The material in this book is based on the Frank Lowe Lectures at the Bartlett School of Architecture. These architects' talks were originally set up to surprise the audience with the exposure of a certain taste or affinity, or to provide them with revealing personal quirks and anecdotes that might have been edited out of an exhibition, catalogue or book. Despite her famous 'Gothic' appearance for example, Odile Decq (a latter-day Juliette Greco in some ways) comes across as an eminently straightforward personality with a private liking for the British atmosphere. In the case of Helmuth Richter, a certain initial shyness coupled with a resemblance to an astronaut acts as a foil to his considerable dry wit, and his undeniable talent as a designer. Within the academic forum, these outsiders also provide a challenge to sitting faculty members: the cosiness of any city – even London – is no substitute for the cross-fertilisation that is architecture's greatest potential asset.

The book attempts to provide a picture of the interaction between a diverse group of architects working within what we might call the 'inventive' stream of current architecture. Many of the personalities involved know of each other, and several are good friends. Or should we say, allies? Out there in the larger world is a mass of work that is neither merely 'commercial' nor 'local' and nor is it 'pragmatic', but most of our speakers would criticise it for being thoughtless, formally lazy or unchallenging.

A sub-plot of these writings is the opportunity to compare cultures. Four people from the former Soviet Union were deliberately inserted into an otherwise predominantly Western menu. Three are Muscovites, exposed to the world through the 'Paper Architecture' shows of the 1980s; the fourth is their friend Vilen Kunnapu from Talin in Estonia. Immediately we are involved in speculations about influence and networking: if Estonia has a linguistic and cultural affinity with Finland and points west, who is it that Kunnapu is addressing with his architecture? In the same way, one has the feeling that Eric Moss, despite the Angelino character of his work, is as much informed by his close friendship with Co-op Himmelblau (with whom he shares a studio from time to time) as by that with Thom Mayne and Frank Gehry. The precise nature of the built explosion and the audacious object creeping out from the unsuspecting carcass might differ, but the spirit is the same – these men know each other's psychology just as they know their party pieces.

Generational categories are equally fluid. It is clear, for example, that Mike Webb and Neil Denari occupy a corner of twentieth-century effort that few others have the talent to enter. To them, a level of affinity with the machine/the armature/the device never need concern itself with style and hardly ever with placement, and the appropriateness of move-upon-move comes out of an internal logic of interdependent parts. Denari came to know Cedric Price and old Archigram people, and to realise that he had a great fan club amongst English students, whilst he was still a 32-year-old fringe figure in the USA. The conversations flowed easily from then on.

If Arata Isozaki was a key to the mutual exposure and subsequent friendships of English, French, American and Japanese inventive architects – especially in the 1980s – and the late Alvin Boyarsky was another, then Lebbeus Woods (operating from a resource that has until recently boasted no office or school) is certainly a third. His work is accessible on many levels. The famous drawings are so explicit, so full of nuance, detail and thrust, that much of his passion comes forward through his published work – the avenue through which he is known to many. In person, he is full of the same passion, never mincing his words. Admired by Moss, Morphosis and Himmelblau, he is also supported by many young architects who see him as a fearless explorer, and a believer in the power of form and the necessity for it to act for the good of mankind. His midwestern faith shines out and his drawing arm gyrates to a purpose. After a bout of Lebbeus we cannot just sit on our past achievements – he inspires us to get off our backsides and zap back to the drawing board or mouse and press on.

In the present climate, the immense offerings of soft technology and a general search for morally justifiable nonchalance ally themselves with a certain (curious) apologetic attitude on the part of architects. It's an opportunistic buck-for-a-yard world out there, so we should seek to create a more thoughtful foundation for architecture. Particularly in American circles, this ambition has resulted in a generation of young architects who are well read in the works of French philosophy and communications theory being plunged out of graduate school into an air-conditioned machine for making well-sealed sheds. In Britain, however, the philosophers still don't help much: confronted with uncle's garage or Mum's dayroom you are forced to think about the more practical matters of logic, form and construction. So let's try to redefine what we're about by attempting to establish a true intellectual base for architecture – without the impedimenta of physical objects.

## stan allen

## Material Practices: Architecture After Semiotics

National Diet Library,
Kansai Kan, Competition, 1996

Postmodernism in architecture is usually associated with a rediscovery of the past. However, an equally important shift preceded, and in many ways underwrote, the Postmodern turn to the past. It was a response not only to a call for a reinscription of architecture into history, but also to a contemporary demand for meaning in architecture. History provided a ready-made catalogue of 'meaningful' forms, but in order for the past to be appropriated and utilised, it had to be detached from its original context and converted into a sign.

But once architecture's signifying capacity had been opened up, no limit could be placed on signified content. 'History' is but one of the many things that a semiotic architecture can signify. The Postmodern turn toward a semiotic architecture at the end of the 1960s and the beginning of the 1970s has itself been subject to intense critical scrutiny, from both a formal and an ideological point of view. But I would like to suggest that even the most radical critiques have left intact the fundamental assumption that architecture forms a discursive system. Meaning today may be multiple, contested, contaminated and partial, but meaning is still the issue.

But an architecture that works exclusively in the semiotic register and defines its role as critique, commentary, or even 'interrogation' (a laying bare of the intricacies of architecture's complicity with power and politics) has, in some fundamental way given up on the possibility of intervening in that reality. Under the dominance of the representational model, architecture has surrendered its capacity to imagine, to propose, or to construct alternative realities. As Robin Evans has remarked, a building was once 'an opportunity to improve the human condition'; now it is understood as 'an opportunity to express the human condition'. Architecture is perceived as a discursive practice, whose specific capacities are utilised to express, to critique or to make apparent the hard realities of a world that is held safely at arm's length.

In my current work, by contrast, architecture is conceived as a material practice, that is to say, as an activity that works in and amongst the world of things, and not exclusively with meaning and image. It is an architecture dedicated to concrete proposals and realistic strategies of implementation and not to distanced commentary or critique. These projects mark a return to instrumentality and a move away from the representational imperative in architecture. Material practices, (ecology,

urbanism or engineering, for example) are concerned with the behaviour of large-scale assemblages over time. They do not work primarily with images or meaning, or even with objects, but with performance: energy inputs and outputs, the calibration of force and resistance. They are less concerned with what things look like and more concerned with what they can do. Although these material practices work instrumentally, they are not limited to the direct manipulation of given material. Instead, they project transformations of reality by means of abstract techniques such as notation, simulation or calculation. Material practices organise and transform aggregates of labour, materials, energy and resources, but they work through necessarily mediated procedures, which leave their trace on the work.

What I am proposing here is not a simple return to the now discredited certainties of high modernism (although at times I may come suspiciously close). I would make two claims in particular. The first is that architecture's instrumentality can be reconcieved, not as a mark of modernity's demand for efficient implementation but as the site of architecture's contact with the complexity of the real. By immersing architecture in the world of things, it becomes possible to produce what Jean-François Lyotard has referred to as a 'volatile, unordered, unpoliceable communication that will always outwit the judicial domination of language'. The second claim is for a practice engaged in time and process – an architecture devoted not to the production of autonomous objects, but rather to the production of directed fields in which programme, event and activity can play themselves out.

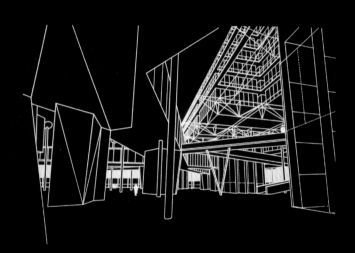

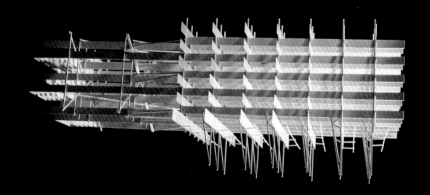

Barcelona ZAL Competition, 1996:
stitch map (top)

National Diet Library, Kansai Kan,
Competition, 1996:
detail of model – entry and lobby
(middle left)

Perspective: reading room and
exposed stacks (middle right)

Study model – structural stack
element (bottom)

## PROJECT DESCRIPTIONS
### Barcelona ZAL

Patches and Corridors: Borrowing a concept from landscape ecology, the given surface area of the site is organised into 'patches' and 'corridors'. Patches are defined as non-linear surfaces – in this case either green areas where a return to indigenous habitat is encouraged, or built-up areas to accommodate the new programmes. Corridors are infrastructural pathways containing movement, services and programme. The superposition of these two systems creates a mosaic of natural and artificial surfaces. Taking an optimistic view of the future of the site, this project anticipates the participation of different architects, agencies and individuals. By creating a structured field condition that is architecturally specific yet programmatically indeterminate, the future life of the site is free to unfold beyond the fixed limits of a master plan.

### National Diet Library, Kansai Kan

Information Landscape: The public spaces of the library are located at ground level in continuity with the man-made landscape. Instead of a traditional civic space separated from nature, the reading rooms are seen as the extension of the landscape, a vast information garden. New technologies allow the distribution and exchange of information without the weighty apparatus of traditional institutions.

Visible Storage: We wanted the users of the library constantly to feel the presence of the vast quantity of material stored in the library. By updating the technology of the 'Snead Stack System' (self-supporting stacks with lightweight walkways for access) we can accommodate the circulating collection in a dense structural matrix occupying the very centre of the building, visible to the readers and researchers within.

Loose Fit: The envelope of the building is loosely drawn around the programmes, distributed without hierarchy over the built area of the site. An informal separation between the site and the events housed within is formed. Partial transparencies reveal the mismatch of container and contained. These residual spaces allow a programmatic indeterminacy where the function of the library can be extended or supplemented by new collective programmes.

**Credits**
Barcelona ZAL:
Competition, 1996
Stan Allen Architect,
assisted by:
Adriana Nacheva
Céline Parmentier
Troels Rugjberg
Nona Yehia

National Diet Library:
Competition, 1996
Stan Allen Architect,
assisted by:
Tsuto Sakamoto
Troels Rugjberg
Mieko Sakamoto

A firm of four partners is unusual. So how do we operate as an office and how have we survived the last nine years since we began? As much as any philosophical statement, this is the story of our architecture.

There are certain fundamental precepts for starting a successful business. Unfortunately no-one told us beforehand.

## Axiom 1: Healthy Economy
The deep recession of the early 1990s was disastrous but taught useful lessons. The late summer of 1989 was not a good time to open an office – no time probably ever is.

## Axiom 2: Working Capital
Availability of credit is fundamental to survival. Think twice before opening an office with minimal working capital from a competition win and an overdraft facility from the Allied Irish Bank. Gold Card credit is handy, but don't push your luck.

## Axiom 3: Low Overheads
The Kitchen Table office. Sensible, but rejected. The alternative: a West End studio – a different level of ambition (or foolhardiness). In any event try to ensure that your rent is less than your turnover. We quickly moved on from Charlotte Street.

## Axiom 4: Assured Workload
Competition success is a traditional starting point for many firms. Success in three ideas competitions in Birmingham in 1989 was the spur to start up. None of them were realised.

## Conditions of Engagement 1: Remember You Are an Expert
Architects are trained to solve problems, not to specialise. In the design and construction of buildings, surely we are all experts. Our expertise is in architecture. Exhibit your expertise. Grasp opportunities. Find Continuing Professional Development in the everyday. Since 1987 the practice has been involved in teaching at UCL and currently runs a unit in the Diploma School.

## Conditions of Engagement 2:
## Make the Most of Every Opportunity
Size isn't important ... but it helps. All projects offer an opportunity to examine and develop an architectural proposition. Projects may be very different in scale and architectural opportunity offered. Do not turn away work lightly. A wide range of clients and projects informs the discussion.

## Conditions of Engagement 3:
## The Value of Losing Competitions
10 years, 40 competitions, 18 places, 12 wins. You learn more from the ones you lose.

## Conditions of Engagement 4:
## If It Isn't Drawn It Can't be Discussed
Establish a mode of discussion that subordinates the individual ego to the identity and life of the project. Drawings are our vehicle for discussion.

## Conditions of Engagement 5:
## Never Work for Family or Friends
... unless you have to. Most of our early projects came via family and friends. Family remains family. Friendships have been tested.

## Conditions of Engagement 6:
## There's No Such Thing as Bad Press
Engage shamelessly with the media – whether advertising in the classified section of the local paper or appearing on breakfast-TV game shows.

## Conditions of Engagement 7:
## Remember to Keep in Touch
Old clients, other architects, school friends, complete strangers. The source of new work is always unexpected and surprising.

## Conditions of Engagement 8:
## Shadow (Gap) Boxing

The shadow-gap detail as opposed to the cover strip has not only represented the holy grail for many modern architects but has become an unfortunate architectural shorthand for Modernism. Try a more relaxed and appropriate approach to details. For each project there is a process of understanding and identifying available opportunities. For each guiding idea behind a project there is a key detail that is crucial to the manifestation of that idea. Consider the sequence and method of construction at full size. The dirty-fingermark syndrome has become a hallmark of white Minimalism and the illusory detail.

## Conditions of Engagement 9:
## Occupation

The process of occupation of buildings is one over which architects have no prescriptive control – it is this very inhabitation that is, to us, the most instructive and surprising part of the process.

# wiLL aLsop

## Essay by Neil Spiller

Projects and proposals must not be afraid of lying outside the terms of RECOGNITION AND COMPREHENSION of the client and society. It is our job to see beyond those limitations through the process of AESTHETIC INQUIRY. It is the ARCHITECT'S task to bring the work into a value system that will enable society to allow it to exist. This inevitably means compromising in some form to reach an agreement, but this process can be dynamic and creative. If this is not achieved, the work will only exist in the mind of the architect and will be called AVANT-GARDE. This is a different reality that ultimately does not help create the more open attitude towards the built environment that makes the AVANT-GARDE irrelevant.
— Will Alsop 'The Context for Practice' AD PROFILE No.123, 1996

During the 1970s and early 1980s, Alsop's work was little known outside the cognoscenti who hung out in the hallowed Georgian grandeur of the Architectural Association in London. It was through his project for the Riverside Studios in Hammersmith, made in conjunction with Alsop's then partner, John Lyall, that he first achieved public exposure. The curling and twirling of the proposed building's out-of-control balustrading combined with its stripy facade-work launched the pair firmly into the 'to be watched' bracket. Unfortunately it was to be a project not built but admired, and indeed mimicked, by many a student at the time. Along with his proposal for Hamburg city centre this project pushed Alsop out of the avant-garde. It gained him respect as an architect, but perhaps more importantly as an urban designer.

The design of the Hamburg Project was instigated by huge, vibrant, daubed and dripping canvases. Its vivacity dragged urban design proposals out of their traditional uninspired mire into a world of joy, fun and unpredictability, beautiful in its sheer gaudy guts. Essentially it comprised a series of movable roofs and catwalks that enclosed or facilitated a set of events, some foreseen, some unforeseen. Like his mentor, Cedric Price, Alsop 'aims to miss'. Such 'catalytic' structures have become one of Alsop's primary architectural gambits. His formal lexicon features weird, extruded, double-curved banana shapes, often swaddled in heroic-dynamic structural metalwork. His work is flagrant in its formal bravado, but careful and well considered in its programmatic inclusivity. Everything seems allowable in an Alsop structure. Not

for him the anal quest for aesthetic and programmatic purity. Nor does his work sink into obsession with highly wrought detail. His preoccupations do not reside in the beautiful gasket or the delicately turned flange. The buildings are muscular, powerful, and expedient in their detailing.

Cardiff Bay Visitors Centre is another iconic building that has entered the mythology of the architectural profession, supposedly inspired by the shape of Alsop's cigarette lighter.

Rare for an architect with a recognisable aesthetic, Alsop is very interested in issues of community and consultation. His architecture is a genial tool, a toy for communities to embrace, use and change. Above all, Alsop is an artist with a social conscience. His buildings do not accept the status quo but subvert the staid ideological conservatism that so characterises city burghers. His buildings are profoundly humane and diverse.

Alsop's work has recently become more widespread and his celebrity status is assured, yet he strives ever onward – more and more formally dextrous and socially daring. Now in practice with Jan Störmer, he has also joined forces with Roger Zogolovitch to create an urban design consultancy that combines Alsop's architectural skills with those of financial proactivity. We can expect a whole series of innovative urban designs that exploit these strengths.

Alsop and Störmer are currently redesigning Blackfriars Bridge in London, a favourite site for student architectural projects. It features delicately arching columns, an undulating roofscape, an undercroft that suggests a snake's belly and a series of sleek, structural blimps supported on tusk-like columns. Here at last is a bridge/station of which to be truly proud.

## The Difference-Scape:
## Towards a Digital Architecture

Multi-level landscape design

In relation to architectural and spatial practices, the use of digital technologies posits a number of interesting questions regarding notions of utility, conceptual artifice and representation. Even if we think of the computer as a 'neutral' tool, embedded into the complex procedures of design, it is essentially still capable of dismantling our conventional modalities of making, reading, writing, communicating and, inevitably, comprehending. Digital technology – the foundation of computing, the Web, the mass media and a vast array of other so-called 'advances' – is no less a tool of expression, and form-giver to desire, than it is a socio-political instrument. Another entirely different view might suggest that the digital is bringing on a new landscape delineated by those who have access and those who don't – one group embracing the twenty-first century while the other becomes a dangerous new underclass.

The digital makes it possible to operate simultaneously on an infinite array of scales and meanings. One of these is an idea of community, based entirely on the scope of our access to information. We strive to be simultaneously 'located' within and 'dislocated' from a 'community' through the digital interfaces we are conjuring, and yet interaction and, by extension, perception, is now in a constant state of flux where the only emerging landscape is one of difference.

The ability to belong to such a large-scale community where cultural boundaries are physically erased is more often than not accompanied by an attempted erasure of cultural identity. In the end, however, emphasis is not necessarily placed on the common ground shared by diverse factions, but on the opportunity to decipher precisely the opposite. For instance, through a reading of a given culture's misappropriations of another one, it is actually possible that one could begin to measure difference. A good example of this is Japan's sense of its own cultural and iconographic make-up as a mediated reflection of American and Western European pop culture. Elvis, Marilyn, Superman, Tintin and the like are absorbed, reworked and distributed globally in various forms and embodiments ranging from Manga to Bullet Trains. The icons that make up this new landscape of difference are essentially an array of mediated reflexes of similitude and diversification mirrored endlessly over networks, an infinity of 'home-pages' and global, televised images.

To digress somewhat, the notions of modernity that essentially emerged from pre- and post-war Western Europe called for a fabricated perfection that was instigated in part from an overt and obsessive interest in hygiene, homogeneity and the relentless export of ideals. The International Style in architectural and design circles was a deliberate and perfectly engineered marketing ploy. In many ways the hype that surrounds the Web has some remarkable similarities. It is essentially being peddled as a place where we are all happily plugged in, having access to infinite flows of information, forming utopian communities on the fringes with the ability to access goods, thoughts, sex, news, lifestyles and just about anything we desire. The Web is purported to be clean, pristine, open and free, a new terrain for all those with an access code. Millions can meander freely, pursuing their every whim. And all this is ostensibly without censorship, persecution, fears of reprisal or confinement of any sort. It is being peddled as the melting-pot without the danger, the communal farm without the sweat, the ultimate vacation without the journey. The hollow promise of a merging, melting global community as a perfect place is still illusory at best.

The digital, in all of its incarnations, can therefore be seen within a space of control where software is a 'predetermining' agent and, conversely, as a territory where the renegade spirit has overrun the mandated and procedural. Ultimately, the truth that belies the potential of the digital is that no matter how entrenched it becomes in our daily lives, it will never be entirely familiar to us. Our distance from the electrosphere will always be a chasm, as far-reaching as the limits of the cosmos. This threshold of knowledge is indisputably insurmountable. However, the impossibility of dominance over the newly manufactured nature and of understanding the

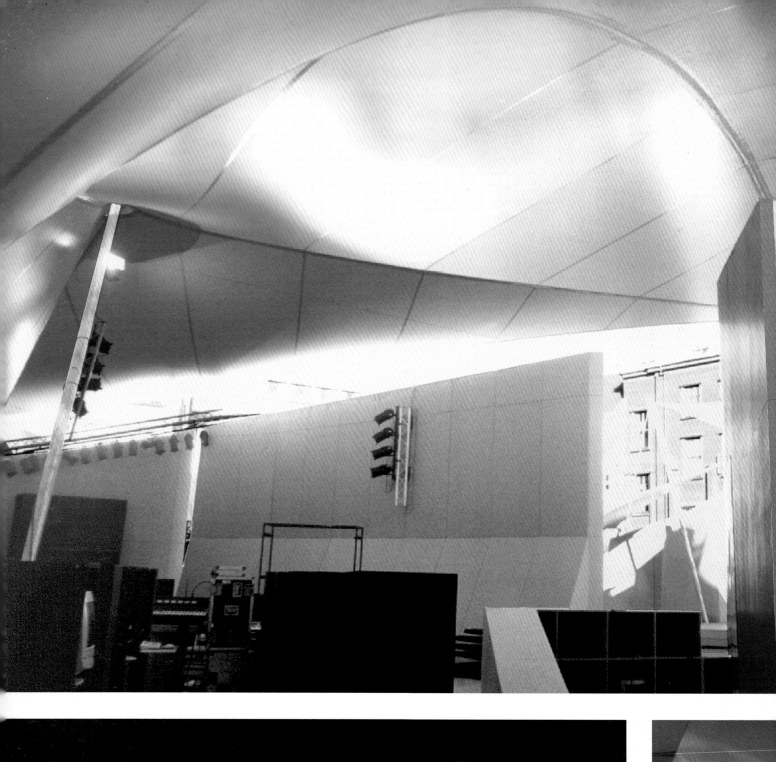
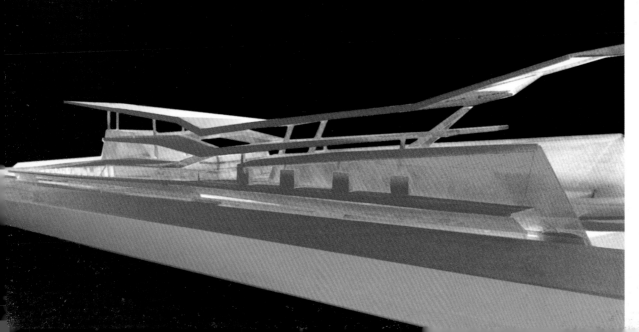

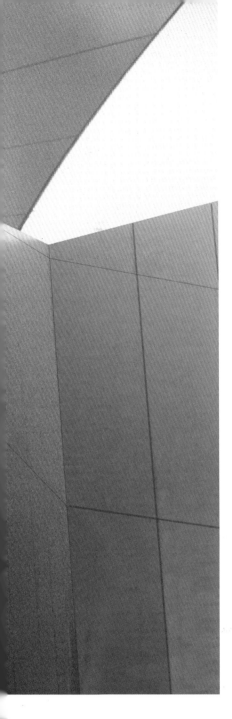

lapses and gaps it entails, is perhaps where the most potential lies for new landscapes that are only beginning to emerge.

Think about a computer for a moment: as you enact a keystroke, a signal goes off somewhere, and in that transmission there is infinite potential – events happen in-between space, time and distance. This is similar to those ancient ships appearing on a distant horizon, imbued with goods, people and, above all, knowledge. Architecture could be seen this way, too – not just through its formal principles, but by its implicit condition as a text of sorts that can interpret and attempt to make sense of the landscape and territories it occupies and forms. The inscriptions we make as architects should be about the human aspiration towards the unknown, manifest most eloquently in what we relentlessly pursue – the space that now begins to enfold us.

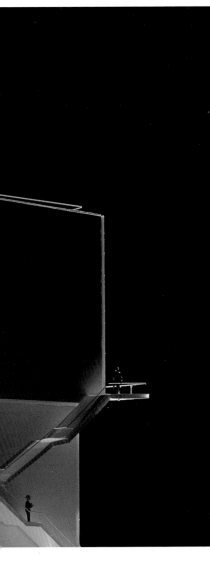

there are wraps of web-like strands and highly considered glazing; there are sheeted entrails of balustrading that seem to skim the faces of the solids as if trying to scamper down (which is exactly what the stairs behind them attempt to do); the caress of detached planes of thin membrane and then, the direct mass of the cinema box.

Straightforwardly, Co-op Himmelblau pack all the cinemas into the box, but on closer inspection, these components are folded together in pairs so as to produce ingenious inner spaces for the public.

As usual in their work, the building defies simple this-and-that description. The typology is so original that the topology becomes simultaneously wild and inevitable. This phase of their work must be described as 'mature' if only because it has taken on board the issue of integration of serial motives without any loss of spark. A stunning challenge to the contemporary 'cool'.

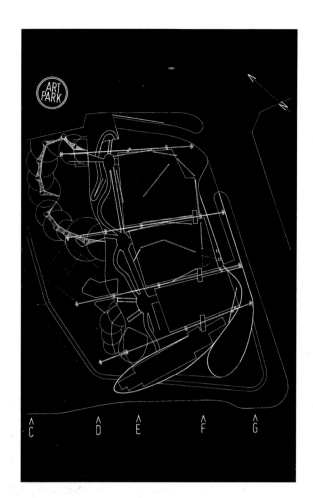

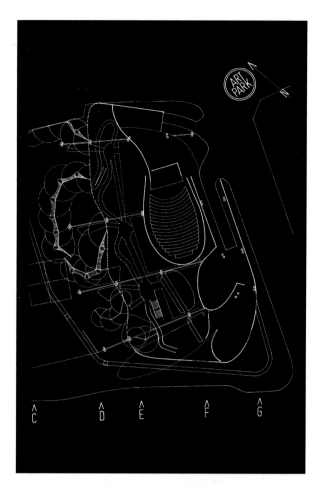

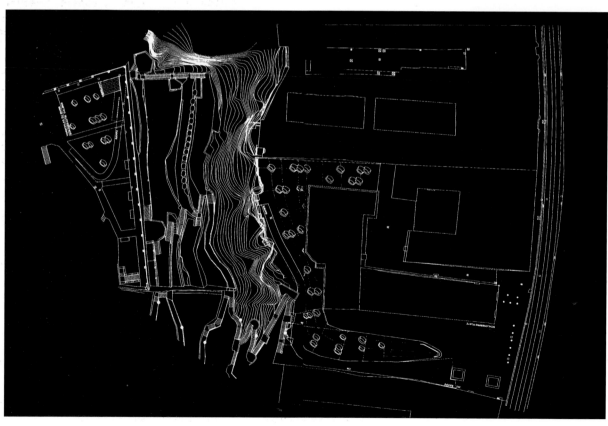

Tongue, Claws and Tail

Museum: Buenos Aires: Ground
and 'Yard' (Claws) (top left)
Museum: Buenos Aires:
Gallery Levels (Claws)(top right)
GRAZ Art Museum (Tongue) (bottom)

Total architecture has always been associated with the Heroic period of the 1920s and 1930s, yet most experimental work of recent years has had to insinuate its way through the nooks and crannies of urban society, appearing not to threaten the established typological models and the fashionable mainstream. Accordingly, one develops a ready inclination to enjoy notions of infiltration, parasitism or surprise revelation. These three projects are the children of this enjoyment.

**Tongue** (Peter Cook/Colin Fournier with David Ardill/David Thompson)
This project is a first-stage response to a crazy combination of forces. First: a small Baroque palace in the centre of Graz that is used as a modern-art museum – the paradox of old fruitiness and new clarity. Second: the sliver of incongruous space between the palace and a small, steep mountain topped by a castle, used for simple gallery space. Third: the intention of using the inside of the mountain for a new-media space – literally a black box. Fourth: the appointment of Peter Weibl, Austria's most energetic, 'hands on' avant-garde figure, as director of the museum. The mix is bizarre, the potential considerable.

Our response is to invent a new architectural element, a continuous membrane called the 'Tongue'. We create a roof to the new spaces and an insertion into the mountain containing all the electrics, electronics, screening and servicing systems and filtered natural light, ready to be mixed or scrambled together by the director of each event or display. A routing system salivates alongside the Tongue, gets into the mountain and leaps up on to the terrace of the castle above, where there can be further 'gallery' spaces. The top of the Tongue erupts into a series of globular rooflights, its tip tantalisingly protruding out into the small public square. It hovers just above the surface of the ground and cheekily points to Gunther Domenig's bridge over the river.

**Claws** (Peter Cook)
The project is a development of the competition scheme for an art museum in Buenos Aires. Frustrated with the traditional uptight series of galleries in a fancy shell, we gained more inspiration from such places as the garden of New York's Museum of Modern Art, the Triennale Gardens in Milan, Kaspar König's 'Von Hier Aus' in Dusseldorf or his Munster sculpture events. Parallel with this is a desire to engage with a key architectural issue for the 2000s: can we invent a new shed-and-yard typology where the inside-outside relationship becomes analogous to the garage-vehicle, the house-garden, the kitchen-restaurant? The opportunity exists to create a new kind of space that involves facility, action, the bursting open of the shed. The public garden alongside the proposed museum in Buenos Aires stimulates this connection. The 'Claws' are a series of tracks, cranes, armatures, sheets, rods, paths that can move in and out of the 'depot'. They collectively act as a fragmented and much-developed version of the Tongue. The idea of the Art Park suggests that plantations could conceal and then reveal all types of electronics, electrics or expandable enclosures. A variety of surfaces (some of them bugged with outlets) sweep by in a casual manner. The act of 'clawing' is key: catching and stimulating space and encouraging the artist's next move.

**Tail** (Peter Cook/Yael Reisner)
A modelled skin that infiltrates my own early 1900s apartment in South Hampstead starts to ricochet out into the garden. So far without 'claws', it is able to wander around desired pockets inside and then meander outside so as to create an evening-sun catcher, tweaking the edge of the garden from time to time and ending as a prototype summerhouse. Tail will continue to develop, as more skin or with more devices sneaking out from it. In this way, the 1930s fascination with the 'garden-infiltrating-house' is reversed. A fragmented alternative to the Mediterranean white courtyard is offered by something that – although Modernist – carries the faint memory of vistas, gazebos and English narrativism.

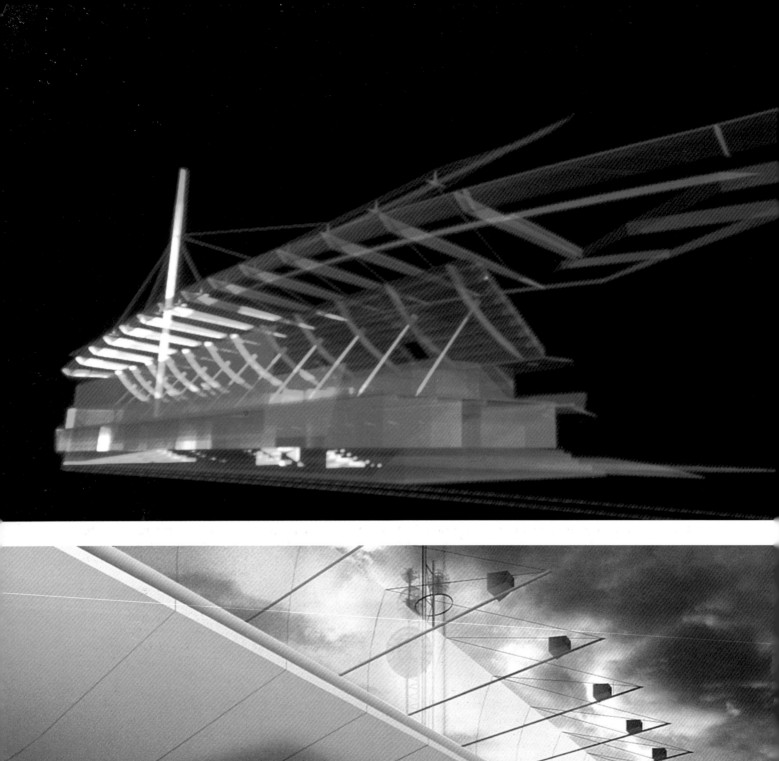

## odiLe decq and benoit cornette

### Hyper Tension

Tribunes, Orleans, 1997 (top)
EPAD-C.E.A. Viaduc, Nanterre (bottom)

Today's society is caught in a moment of complexity and acceleration. Speed, movement and displacement have changed our vision of space, cities and landscape. The rapid development of communication networks compresses time to such an extent that we can no longer build up a clear image of the city or of the living space.

We are all nomads, travelling between reality and unreality. Moving from city to city, sending faxes, channel-surfing, tele-conferencing are all means by which we navigate space and meaning. This globalisation of our society, through the mechanisms of information-exchange and travel-exchange, reconfigures our comprehension of space in motion.

The architecture of these new territories could therefore be perceived as imperfect, unlimited and evolving. Cities and territories are becoming redefined as a network in continuous flux.

Paul Virilio distinguished two orders: that of place, characterised by a stability of form, and that of speed, characterised by the fading of form. The disappearance of defined forms, of precise limits, characterises the evolution of architecture based on movement. Static *quatrocento* perspective can no longer express the chaotic disorder and fragmentation of urban space, nor respond to our new perception of time and space. We must stop thinking in terms of this old notion of centrality. We must think of the world as a topological, apparent disorder that defines new urban forms, spreading over territories in relation to continuity, in discontinuity, deformations, density and dynamic heterogeneity, rather than in relation to a metric system. We must question static spatiality and constancy of forms in time. We must think about the possibility of a new kind of gravity, or machine of gravity, that understands the relativity of perception.

We are now in a dynamic period in which the body is unstable, where time and space are perceived not as permanent, but as instants, as events. We have entered the nomadic era in which the discontinuity of space and the fracture of time is the modern condition.

The necessity of displacement and the movement of the body inside space must be integrated. A succession of points of view generates a dynamic vision of space. This variation of perspectives creates a permanent tension and a sensual, complex ambiguity in the perception of space. The sequential circulation of images such as linear distortion constantly displaces and disturbs one's point of view. We never think in terms of centred space and axes, but in terms of sliding and tangential spaces, of chains of images, to create escaping lines, moving perspectives, sequential images where tension is introduced in the assemblage of fading forms. Architecture and space are a matter of constant discovery and nothing is ever out of bounds.

It is not only a question of shaping, but of how to use the development of technologies and innovations in other fields of research, such as the automotive, aviation, structural calculation, software, etc., in order to build new types of space. The pursuit of lightness, of fluidity, of virtuality, of maximum performance with minimum material could be used to benefit the architecture of today and tomorrow by the development of new structures, envelopes, aerodynamism of forms, lightness of design.

In the BPO (Banque Populaire de l'Ouest) at Rennes the cinematic promenade through the dissociated components of inside/outside creates an in-between space. The hypertrophy of the length of the hall between the glass curtain and the curved glossy wall creates tension and movement inside the space. The strong presence of absence creates ambiguity, fusion and illusion. Space becomes liquid; its limits disappear. The system of layering structure, glass facade and curved wall virtually draws the outside into the inside and vice versa. The facade not only closes the inner space to the outside, but creates a space itself: the depth of the facade. The discovery of space through movement, the understanding of a dimension of space through displacement, the ambiguity of spatial limits, stimulates the perception of the hall, which must be travelled to be understood and valued on its own terms.

In the motorway bridge and control building at Nanterre, behind La Defense, the thin steel piles of the bridge supporting the large concrete span create an inversion by dynamically optimising the engineering. The curved design of the concrete span skews the view under the bridge. The building itself is detached from the ground, hanging on the arches of the bridge. This structure, which belongs to the world of the motorway and would otherwise have been oppressed by it, thus finds itself in a dominant position over the park. Though it is immobile, through its position and its design it absorbs the dynamism and the symbolism of motorway speed and movement, appearing like a cursor suspended on a line.

In the control tower of Bordeaux Airport the aim was to maximise the impression of lightness, to give the control room on top the sense of having escaped gravity, of belonging to the aerial field. The displacement of the stable point and the discussion of the constituent elements of the tower (two lifts, a staircase and a double shaft) enables rearticulation in a tripod structure, the control room floating on a cantilever over the runway.

In the rugby stadium at Orleans the horizontal dissociation of the different levels of floor and of the suspended cover, amplified by their sliding structure and the asymmetric suspension, gives the project the impression of displacement and movement, in a reference to the energy and power of rugby itself.

# neiL denari

Vertical Weekly Mansion, Tokyo, 1994–96
Gallery MA (Interrupted Projections) Tokyo, 1996

## Vertical Weekly Mansion (Housing Hi-Rise Prototype), Tokyo 1994–96
Client: Nippon Housing International, Ltd.
Budget: $ 5.0 mil USD (Proposal)
Assistants: Irene Lai, Gunther Schatz, John Hartmann

Weekly mansions are existing types of temporary housing in Tokyo. Normally structured as multi-storey, single-loaded, corridor-slab buildings, they maximise land value by providing fluctuating residences for itinerant salarymen at extremely high monthly rents. The convenience of this type of housing, usually located within the centre of Tokyo or its immediate periphery, allows companies or universities to mobilise their workforce easily.

As Tokyo's land area must be vertically expanded, the 30-metre-high Vertical Weekly Mansion ('mansion' being one of the more humorously misapplied loan words in Japan) is a building projected for a 54 m$^2$ footprint in the Aoyama sector of Tokyo, home to many corporate headquarters such as c-ITOH and Honda. Eight repetitive floors of one-room apartments are stacked between an entrance space on the ground level and a two-level, multi-purpose/bar space at the top. In the basement level, space is divided between a public bar in front and the service areas (laundry and trash compaction) in the back.

Largely functionally determined, this project is indeed Straight Forward Architecture. The zoning envelope in Tokyo allows a vertical extrusion up to 30 metres. Above that, the building mass must slope back by 45 degrees. In this situation, there is no room to slope back above the site perimeter. Floor-area ratios, budgets, structure, strict earthquake codes, etc., all determine the conventional building in Tokyo. This Hi-Rise Prototype asserts difference by treating the interior apartment as an industrial design where futons and aluminium tables are concealed in the floor surface for temporary pop-up use. Each apartment contains video projection and flat-screen Liquid Crystal Display wall panels.

A reinforced-concrete service core acts as the main column, with steel-framed floors and bracing for the units. Steel stairs are cantilevered from the rear side of the concrete core. Electron-inverting glass and aluminium panels are the main external cladding materials.

## Gallery MA (Interrupted Projections), Tokyo 1996
Client: Gallery MA / TOTO
Budget: $80,000 USD (Completed 1996)
Assistant LA: Georg Kolmayr
Assistants Tokyo: Sei'ichi Kozu, Masaaki Oka

Sited above the Nogizaka subway station in Tokyo, Gallery MA, by Cor-Tex Architecture, is an eleven-year-old space devoted to exhibiting architecture and related design. The project was inserted into the third floor of a six-storey building, where half of the ground-floor footprint stops to provide a courtyard bounded by concrete walls and the buildings beyond. A glass membrane divides the interior space from the courtyard and allows total visual invasion into the inserted project. The space is roughly 6.5 x 11 metres in plan and 2.45 metres in section. The experimental space itself is the project's programme.

The space is developed from the Homolosine Interrupted Projection Mapping System, which depicts the world in a series of sheared ellipses. Thus the green surface inside Gallery MA is an 'interrupted projection' for it deploys a flattened and empty global surface to form space. This bends and loops to form a three-dimensionally smooth yet complex geometry capable of merging with the graphic world of visual codes and conventional signs. This is the WORLDSHEET, covered with logos of fictional companies such as OVERCODES or UNIVOCAL. Each has a bar code next to it, which triggers information on to a hand-held camera/screen called the NAVICAM, a device in development by SONY.

Vertical Weekly Mansion

## foreign office

New Grounds

In the competition for the Yokohama International Port Terminal, the identification of the ground and the enveloping surfaces became consistent, partly because we were simply carrying forward already existing research on surfaces as structural devices, partly due to the fact that the programme of the project, a transportation facility, was more suited to the exploration of a shifting, unstable construction of the ground.

The structural qualities of the ground in this project came much closer to the idea of a hollowed ground where loads are not distributed by gravitational force through columns, but rather by displacing stresses through the surface of the shell. This shell-like structure also became a potential solution to the lateral loads frequently produced by seismic movements in Japan. The particular condition of the Japanese ground, where non-gravitational stresses are often more punishing than gravitional ones, became clearly instrumental as this development progressed. The main zones of structural rigidity appear here parallel to the direction of the folds, rather than in the edges of the cuts. The reason for this was the predominant direction of the circulatory flow, along the longitudinal direction of the project. The removal of the structure away from the cuts, the bifurcations of the surface, was necessary because they also had to become points of physical access. But beyond the functional requirements, this shift also meant a higher degree of integration between the surface and its static properties: these were produced as true singularities of the shell rather than as structural elements embedded in its accidents. From a hybridisation of types, the crucial step here was to move to a strategy of differentiation of a tectonic system: the folded surface.

Another project was a consultancy for a large multi-modal transportation in Pusan, Korea. The aim was to connect the city to the developing waterfront by means of a 120,000 m², high-speed rail terminal, plus bus station and associated car-park. The spatial structure of the tracks became a crucial figure as the need to keep the station operative during the construction of the new terminal forced us to incorporate these traces into the spatial structure of the project itself. Seeking to turn the station into a new public space that would connect ground level with the station concourse at +8.5 metres and with a whole new city – 800,000 m² floor area – built over the tracks at +15,00 metres the building would dissolve into a new plaza and the road infrastructure

serving the complex. The dissolution of the building into the infrastructural elements that project beyond the 'frame' of the site became the most remarkable development in respect to the construction of a new ground, formally and functionally blending the building and the ground. The 'frame' is thereby extended even beyond the limits of the legal ground, by melting topographic and programmatic conditions between the project and its frame. This moves one step further in terms of the relation between figure and ground.

The topography we proposed was a shredded surface, linking the different levels by weaving undulating bands to provide access, light and ventilation to the concourse and the platforms. The structure of the bands was produced using a series of arches and catenaries, whose geometries determine the undulations of the bands of ground/envelope.

A speculative competition for a 'Virtual House' allowed us to test the same set of ideas on an entirely different scale. The project here was to operate with an abstracted band of ground – a band of 'disruptive pattern material' – to produce organisations alternative to the conventional compartmentalisation of domestic space. Here, the manipulation of the ground differs from past experiments in which we maintained the orientation of the surface in respect to gravity. In the Virtual House that relationship keeps reversing, each face of the surface shifting constantly between a 'lining' and a 'wrapping' condition. A diagonal shift in the plan increased the spatial complexity of the structure, making possible the stacking of different units to enable the unlimited proliferation of the body of the house.

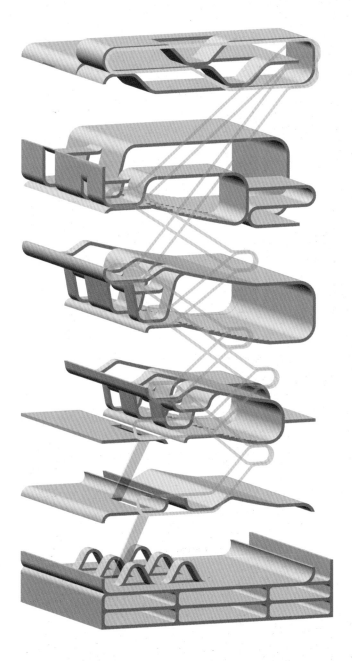

The hollow ground that we have been developing through the research, acquired in this project a more paradigmatic state where the possibility to proliferate the structure is an alternative development to the 'unframed' quality of the ground that we had explored through the previous projects.

To summarise the qualities of these emerging 'new grounds':

1. They are fundamentally active, operative in nature, and closer to the contemporary conception of platforms as operative systems than to the classical one of pediments or bases aimed at the framing, neutralisation and erasure of the field of operation, which were intended to produce an ideal background for architecture to become a readable figure.

2. They move away from the determining condition of 'site' as a kind of natural condition. New grounds are not natural – physically or culturally – but are artificially constructed.

3. They are neither abstract nor neutral and homogeneous, but concrete and diverse.

4. They have an uncertain framing, for the field in which they exist is not a fragment but a differentiated domain affiliated to external processes. They are not separable from the operation we produce on them.

5. They are neither a datum nor a reference.

6. They are neither solid nor structured by gravity, but are hollow and 'diagonally' structured.

## VOLKER GIENCKE

Pushing the Borderline

In 1960 Yves Klein, the painter of space, flung himself into the void: 'On this day I started to hate the birds which were flying criss-cross over the sky, because they tried to make holes into my most beautiful and magnificent work ...' Klein strove for a space without boundaries or temporal constraint. By symbolically 'signing' the sky he declared 'monochromy' to be the fundamental concept of his painting.

When looking down on the earth from an aeroplane it appears two-dimensional. From high above, mountains and valleys become planes. Not even one's knowledge that rivers flow down makes these patterns look three-dimensional. As we can see, knowledge alone is not sufficient to gain access to the truth. Direct lighting, which casts shadows, reveals that a surface has depressions and elevations. Like the landscape, architecture loses its three-dimensionality and becomes facade.

The areas we build up, no matter whether they are soil, flat land or steep slopes, are all places for ever embedded in a particular geographic and topological 'clothing'. Man's work has changed these conditions – sometimes improved them, sometimes destroyed them, though more often the latter has happened. A quarry is like a view into the interior of the earth: the ground opens. A path, a street, hurt the soil like cuts. These artificial interventions need not necessarily destroy nature but – from a more positive point of view – may also reformulate it. A highway in the landscape can be something great, even if it was built as part of a work-creation programme (as happened in the 1930s in Germany).

There are places and landscapes with a magical atmosphere that is very hard to describe. These are the places to which one always returns, the places that are always remembered. The history of mankind is like the history of a city – always one of location, landscape and geography.

Let us assume that the same technological capacity and the same amount of invested capital could allow a uniform architectural standard all over the world. If this were the case, the criteria that would make a location unmistakable – such as beauty of landscape, poetics of location and distinctive architecture – would become very significant. Under these conditions architecture, understood as an artificial environment, a 'work of art', takes on a special role. It must be better than that which nature and history have created.

The freedom of architecture is the freedom of art. Art assumes that all problems are solved, that art itself is the solution to problems that, in fact, never existed. I am decisively against the non-differentiation between art and life, against its fragmentation, because art can only be radical by being art (as a transformed reality, as an illusion). Sensuality, fantasy, intellect and creativity are complementary to the daily grind of society. The revolutionary potential of art lies in the assumption that it alone can satisfy the non-materialistic needs of mankind.

It is an anthropological phenomenon to do everything systematically – to take away the meaning of the unconscious, the unspeakable, invisible, transcendental – in order simultaneously to deplore the loss of fascination and the secretive. In the utter meaninglessness of this world everything could be aesthesia, everything could be explained by sexuality, everything is politics, art, architecture. But if everything is aesthesia, then nothing is beautiful anymore and nothing is ugly. If everything is sexual, sexuality loses its determinative strength. If everything is architecture then, at the same time, nothing is architecture.

The new building at the Louvre could be defined as an excellent supermarket, as a 'perfect' building as far as the media and advertising are concerned. Or one could see the Grand Arc in La Defense as hyper-realistic architecture and therefore belonging to the world of fairy tale. I stand there open-mouthed but without enjoyment. My passion evaporates in view of this perfection like butter in the sun. Then I remember a sentence from Cedric Price: 'A city can be wonderful, when driving through it, and it can be terrible, if one has to die in it.' And suddenly everything is relative again, and nothing is perfect any more.

## What is contemporary?

So often the contemporary perception of landscape is soft and inarticulate, lacking readability and definition, fluffed-up, brushed-up, flowered-up; all decorative fill. To counterpoint this image there is more and more of a dependence in landscape design on graphics. The two-dimensional representation, the illusion of the straight line and the mathematical constructed curve all act as crutches in the hope of defining a dynamically structured space and therefore being contemporary. This is just another sort of decoration. My work is composed of layers.

## Client/User/Programme

The starting point for any project is the client: their needs and dreams. These notions have been expressed in the programme or scope of works and sometimes through a type of philosophical mission statement.

## Site

The achieving of a *genius loci*. A new landscape needs to be in a site not on it. A project should be born from its site, emerging from the land and the place. The site's ambience, climate, history and environmental structure are a backbone to creating a sense of place. The understanding of the site and its specific qualities is the key to the project being site-specific, that is, finding its own particular sense of place.

I often work with the ground plane. It is the one area people physically touch, see, hear and smell. Up, down, hard, soft, wet, dry, crunch and colour can all be its qualities. The ground plane is the first visible structure to be put in place and allows the vegetation time to mature. If you can succeed in putting a project's essence within the ground plane, the site will hold its own over time. Elements on the site may be changed, but rarely the ground plane.

## Concept

Concept and its relation to ideas is crucial to good design. Concept is the total meaning and feeling that is expressed through a project's physical structure. An idea is the translation of a concept through a physical structure. A rock garden or a water feature are physical ideas; their mere presence is not a concept. Lining up a string of ideas will not communicate a meaning, it will just be another string of designer objects. A concept is expressed through the design of the physical ideas, their relationship and overall presence.

A conceptual work is an expression of an issue about which the designer or artist is concerned, whether emotional, social, political, scientific or physiological. It is something that they are trying to understand or believe and want to express.

A concept will give meaning to a site; it is a soul, an essence, that exudes from the site. It is something that creates a sense of total entity and is often felt, more than it is understood, by the visitor. The end result of any project reflects and contains what is put into the project – the energy, the emotion and the thinking.

Why does a painting or work of art touch you? Something inside you connects with it. It is often an ephemeral quality that words are not able to describe. The artist has put his or her soul in there with strong emotions and thoughts. This meaning is evasive. When perceiving a piece, you feel you are almost in its inner core before it slips away from you again, but you know it's there inside. This intimacy with a piece creates fascination, strength and comfort. Is it that very intimacy that moves people to put a piece of art in their home? Perhaps they want to appropriate the art piece. People also appropriate landscapes because of a connection they have felt. When appropriated, a landscape is often maintained at a much higher level.

Each project contains at least these three layers: Client/User/Programme, Site and Concept. It is essential to carry each one forward to make the project evolve.

Evry Square of Human Rights
Park Terrasson, La Villedieu (inset)

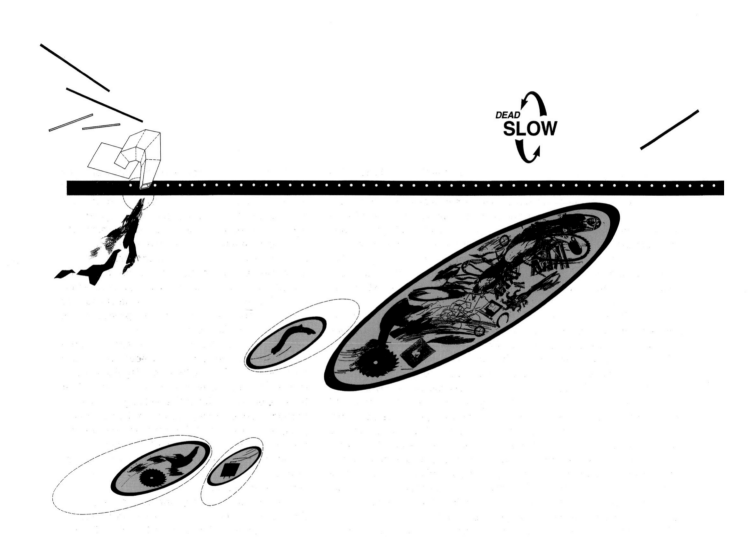

DEAD
SLOW

## jonathan hiLL

### The Institute of Illegal Architects

Frontal Axonometric, Tomb of the
Architect, Production Pace for time,
Institute of Illegal Architects

The term 'architect' is enshrined in law. But who is this law designed to protect? Seemingly, the architect as much as the user. The architectural profession claims a monopoly over specific areas of discourse and practice for the purpose of economic and social self-protection. The primary aim of the profession is to suggest that only the work of architects is entitled to the name 'architecture'. The profession is the police force of architecture. However, the control of architecture by its police is partial and mythical, and a myth sometimes does the most harm to the social group it seems to protect. Professionalism acts as a huge restraint on architects because it encourages them to be parochial and self-absorbed. Ideas and actions that challenge the authority of the profession are marginalised, and consequently, the familiar languages of architectural practice act as a restriction as much as a liberation.

The architect is enshrined in law but architecture has no legal protection. Architects see this situation as a contradiction but it merely recognises that architecture is more than just the work of architects. Some of the most speculative and thoughtful architecture is produced by the 'illegal' architect who may also, for example, be a user, an artist or a surgeon. The illegal architect is, however, not just a person who produces architecture without a professional qualification. The illegal architect questions and subverts the conventions, codes and laws of architecture and therefore can even be a registered architect critical of the profession. Implicit within this argument is the belief that the legal architect can learn from the illegal architect, for whom architecture can be made of anything, anywhere, anyhow, by anyone.

To give my criticism of the architectural profession a tangible target, its focus is the Royal Institute of British Architects. It is common for the institution to be the subject of attack. However, the avantgardist denial of the institutions of art and architecture collapsed on the myth of its own anti-institutionalism, and resulted in either the withering away of radical practice or the incorporation of its depoliticised husk within an expanded discipline. In excepting the original principles of avant-gardism, so many of the seemingly radical projects produced in the last few years have concentrated on the minor. But marginality and the role of the outsider are self-fulfilling. Institutions must be reformed, not destroyed. They are essential to the advocacy of change. Consequently, my proposal is for the construction of an Institute of Illegal Architects.

The relationship between the RIBA and the Institute of Illegal Architects is similar to that between the body and the fairground mirror that distorts the 'original', inviting both laughter and horror. The RIBA incorporates a vertical, hierarchical management structure with precise rules for membership. The Institute of Illegal Architects has no members and consequently no non-members. It is neither Royal, British nor for qualified architects. The Institute of Illegal Architects fosters what the profession omits: the production of architecture by the illegal architect.

The RIBA is located on a corner site in central London at the junction of Weymouth Street and Portland Place. The Institute of Illegal Architects inhabits the public domain of the street rather than the private realm of the building. It is sited in Portland Place, directly in front of the RIBA. Occupying the full width of the street for 250 metres, the Institute blocks the street to vehicular traffic and severs the symbolic route from Regent's Park to Regent Street. It consists of five spaces, each conceived for a specific form of sensual or perceptual production – sound, smell, touch, sight and time – but a tight fit between space and occupation is not expected and is even undesirable. The five zones are hinged around the horizontal plane of the street, so that they appear to be rising from, and sinking into, Portland Place (the highest point is only 1.5 metres above ground level). In addition, the project contains a collection of transient elements, whose number and character are in a constant state of flux. The juxtaposition of these and the five spaces indicates that the seductive power of architecture relies on the accidents of use as much as on the design of the architect, whether illegal or professional.

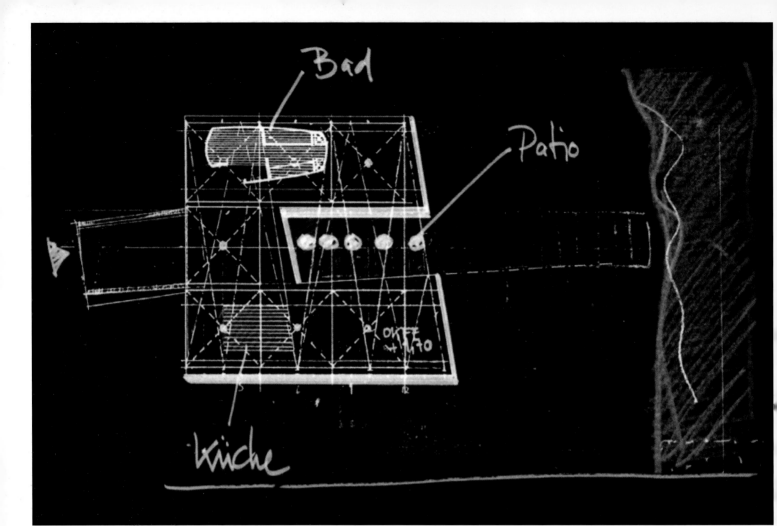

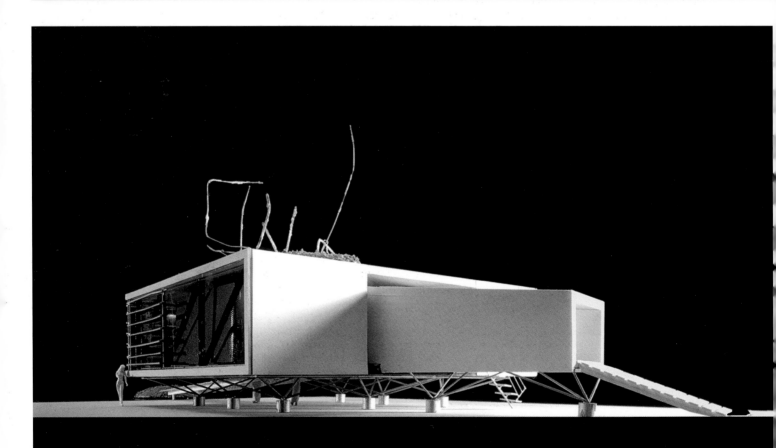

Society develops out of the tension between individual awareness and regulating systems. Personal values come into conflict with the demands of social systems, which subsequently limit the individual. Interaction between private and public is the basis of communication. The increasing appropriation of the private sphere through public media means that spaces for communication are gradually losing their significance. The integrity of the private sphere as a protective membrane has thus been, if not removed altogether, certainly impaired.

We are advocating an architecture that not only houses particular forms of activity and represents them more or less aesthetically, but which also renders social activity and communication transparent so that they are reflected in the architecture itself. This means avoiding motivations that are solely normative, functional or pragmatic since they are all likely to frustrate patterns of communication. The basis of our work is to create a relational network of perceptions, sequences of social movements and programmatic requirements in order to provide an adequate spatial counterpart to communicative action.

Architecture is regarded as an intellectual construction that, among other things, attempts to transform the requirements of the user into space. While the understanding of space is communicated via a complex interplay of elements including acoustic and haptic sensations, its conception and perception is subsumed almost entirely under the visual. Since the image is so predominant, other forms of spatial experience and description are reduced. This visual dependency cuts off the opportunity to employ our own body as a field of reference from which to reconfigure spatial experience and description. Thus, the drawing as the abstraction of space is always a limited means of representation. The basic problem remains of whether spatial determinants could be represented through non-visual models. Whether models of spatial experience not subordinate to the visual exist, or can be developed, is of far-reaching significance for our understanding of space.

We are equally preoccupied with energetic space in the pragmatic execution of architecture. We endeavour to understand a building as a manifestation within an energy field and not merely a specified object to which functions are allocated. This leads us to a different representation of a building's properties. A building interrupts and conducts currents of air and energy. It reflects and absorbs radiation, excludes or accepts the flow of energy, storing and transforming it. Everything is in circulation. A building modifies its environment; the environment modifies the building. When a building casts a shadow, does it belong to the building, or to the area on which it stands, or does it constitute its own dynamic, an autonomous space?

**Gehling House**

This project is envisioned as a temporary structure comprised of prefabricated kit elements that can be dismantled and re-assembled elsewhere. Due to the danger of flooding, the building is elevated on columns. Via large lamellae, more energy enters the house than is released by it. The user can exert a simple, direct influence on the building's energy management by sliding the entire set of shadow-casting, view-defining lamellae along horizontal tracks.

The introduction of a courtyard, complete with trees, sets in motion a dialogue with the exterior space. The courtyard becomes an integral part of the living platform and both act as a stage for selected scenes, which change according to the seasons. At ground level the scene is fragmented; on the living platform just the tree trunks can be seen, and on the terrace, only the treetops. The relationship between exterior and interior spaces is further defined by the adjustable lamellae. The outer skin of the building correlates to the inner functions and uses as defined by the occupant. The chitin shell is transformed into an expressive, faceted skin. The formation and organisation of the facade acts as a communicating filter. Open and closed spaces of communication are in flux depending not only upon the various uses of the spaces but also upon the building's energy needs.

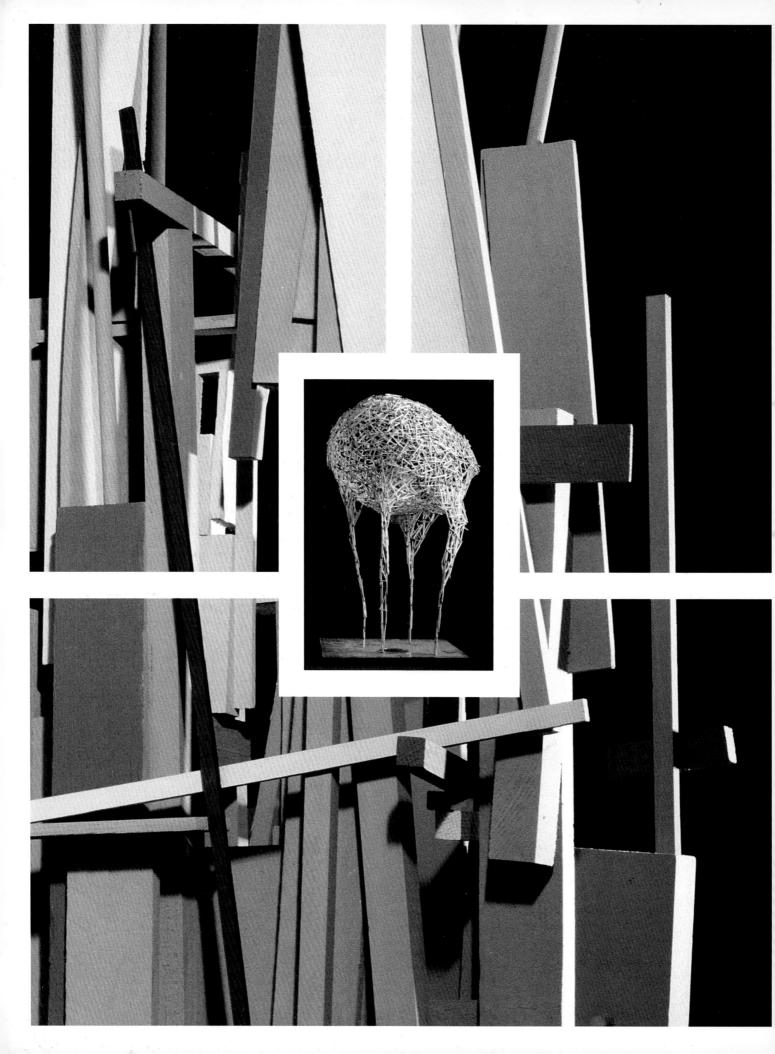

## The Experimental Children's Design Studio, Moscow

The EDAS manifesto, developed over twenty years, is a chaotic but seq-uential stream of thoughts, forming a skeleton on which further ideas can be hung. It is not a system – or it is not precisely described as one. It consists of fragmented notions that allow for interpretation and deviation. It identifies a mechanism that can be dismantled and sub-sequently reassembled, possibly in a different configuration, to reveal something new – perhaps something better. The children express them-selves without the superficial or streamlined presumptions we identify with the adult world. They are drawn to unexplainable things where their imagination is capable of forming super-realistic fantasies.

• The creation of the Experimental Children's Design Studio was not provoked by issues of fashion.

• Developed forms are reinterpreted. This new reality is formalised and recorded.

• The programme is against preconception in any of its forms – only originality is tolerated.

• The aim of the studio is not to create stylistic solutions but to encourage the children to create architectural forms, which are dev-eloped without prejudiced judgements. The children are encouraged to avoid the cultural baggage so endemic in the adult world. Artistic ability is nurtured as the child is encouraged to experiment, to adapt to any stylistic characteristics.

• Clear the essential place in the brain and on the architect's table.

• Universal design skills are developed independently of specific applications, This particularly reflects the nature of the child's creative mentality.

• There is an acceptance of the importance of every stage of sketching and every phase of fluid development from the initial formal idea.

• Traditional notions of basic professional thinking – the Point, the Line, the Flatness, the Volume, the Space – become structure-creating elements.

• There are no mistakes – there are different interpretations.

• Re-evolution of construction – reconstruction of Constructivism.

• Reconstruction is examined through objects.
The OBJECT: any act, gesture, sound, image, fragment, splinter or their combinations within the space of the collage.
The COLLAGE: the condition of the reconstruction.

• A School style is denied.

The School acknowledges free forming; the School acknowledges art experiment.

• The Verbal and the Visual are combined.

• I tell them 'Everything is possible' and at first they do everything – but then they do what is possible.

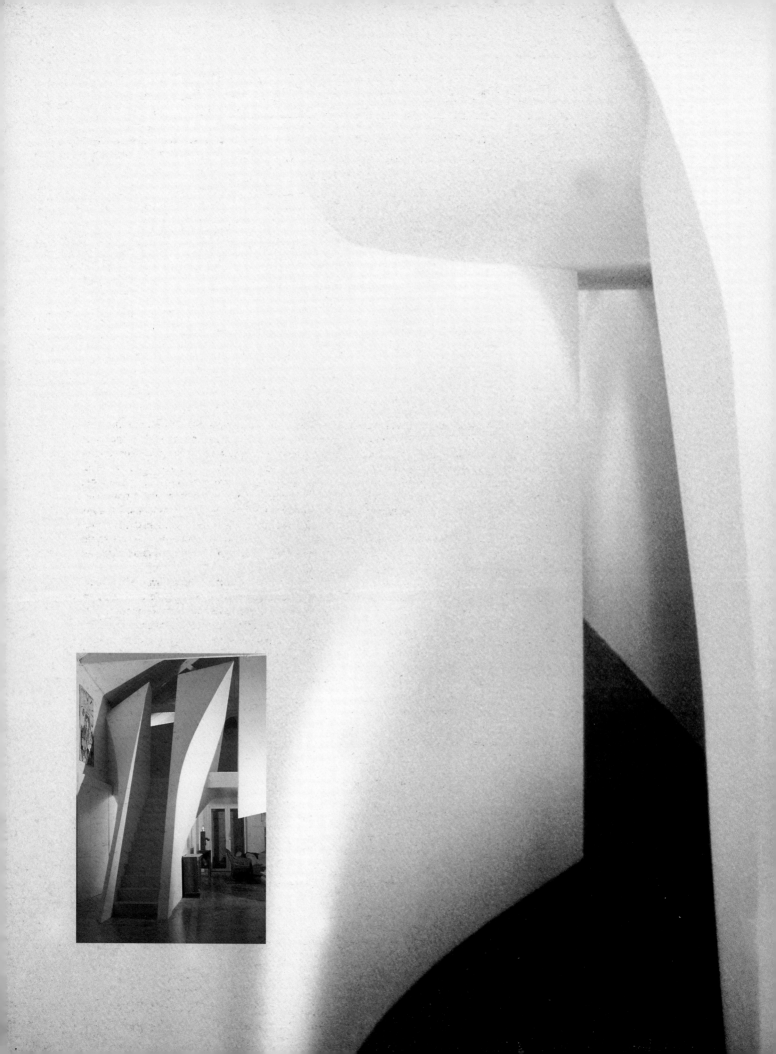

Sapore Restaurant, Melbourne, 1995
Ryan Studio, Melbourne, 1995 (inset)

... The shifting vanishing points, blurred horizon lines, and erased corners are all techniques born of the interior. This is more of a condition of being within than of using or inhabiting the space. The eye is given free reign to travel. At this level we are observing the interior more as a phenomenological installation, testing our ability to perceive space as itself and not as a vessel as, for example, in the saturated colour fields of James Turrell where light is harnessed as a medium.

The translation from minimalist installation art to functional interior is an awkward leap, albeit a brave one. It demands absolute dedication to detail and a ruthlessness aimed towards rejection rather than inclusion. For example, skirtings, door/window frames and cornices are excluded – all devices to cover joins. To achieve the desired result is labour intensive, time consuming and very expensive; a sympathetic client is essential, an unsympathetic one could destroy the result overnight ...
—John Andrews 'Erasing the Corner' in Tom Kovac ARCHITECTURAL MONOGRAPH No. 50

Much of Kovac's work carries with it the suggestion that it is composed of sections of larger, weirder shapes. One can imagine these hyper-forms to be almost anatomical in their complexity. The form of the Gan House in Melbourne (1993), for example, appears to be derived from a vertical section through human mouth parts, lovingly sanded down to a rigorous smoothness. Such associations are crucial to the sensations that Kovac's work provokes. It is at once naturalistic, minimal and expressionist. It is modern yet has historical precedent. Much time and thought appear to have been spent honing forms in order to tread the delicately balanced line between poise and heavy-handedness.

Kovac's architecture may play without disguises, but it has a secret darker life. His sensuous planes conceal a beneath, between, behind and below that come from another place. This is a Piranesi-like world; a concealed geometry of errant, canted, chaotic timber studwork, above which glide Kovac's pristine, polished surfaces. The perfection of the surface guides the concept away from issues of sign, symbol, code and narrative to create a phenomenological vessel almost religious in its belief in its own rightness – its Holy Trinity of light, space and form.

Above all, Kovac's work is an oasis in the Australian metropolis where the normal interplay of light, form and space is temporarily suspended and replaced by a plastic, ubiquitous, twisting, turning surface/vessel that creates an optical machine focused on its own illuminated entrails.

The works straddle many paradoxes. Paradox used to be an insult to the Modernist architect; I see it as a critical component of discussable architecture. The brain is kept moving as much as the eye.

One wonders if in the future Kovac will loosen up a bit and allow his substructure a little more autonomy, perhaps letting it occasionally burst through the perfect plaster to pucker the ubiquitous surface; to show a little more of its scabby ankle. But the work is indeed beautiful and is full of courage and integrity. This is rare in a frenzied, image-addicted world.

# vilen Kunnapu

## The House as Kinetic Sculpture

Group of small houses in Talinn

The house is a kinetic sculpture. It is kinetic because a good deal of movement occurs inside – air, fire, earth, water, people. Water flows in pipes; air where it pleases; people move along corridors, stairs, galleries, roofs and tunnels. Earth is put into pots, from which mysterious trees and bushes emerge. Fire appears from time to time and burns everything down, and the architect begins his eternal, Sisyphean task.

One thing is distinguished from another by its form. A house is made up of form. The process of forming brings the architect infinite pleasure. Forming is the basis of an erotic sense of satisfaction.

The forces establishing a form are various chances and opportunities, prohibitions, papers, faces, bodies; mountains, clouds and rivers, with their innumerable fish, animals and birds. We form a house as if from clay and rejoice that we have staircases, bridges, elevators, escalators, big halls, small rooms, roofs and balconies at our disposal. We imagine little people scurrying like ants along the marvellous pipes that we provide for them.

A pipe is an important image. We know that the inside of the head of a healthy man consists of pipes; that invisible wires come out of his head and connect it with other heads; that a pipe in a house is a symbol that would be difficult, and a pity, to hide.

A quick sketch, a drawing based on intuition, is the foundation of all architecture. It determines almost everything. A sketch provides melody, keynote and rhythm. It lifts a house from the ground. We start a fight against gravity, but fighting gravity is not our final aim: our aim is to fly. One of the first architects to understand this was Vladimir Tatlin. His house as an image was replaced by his image of an aeroplane. He called his aeroplane LETATLIN. His wood and metal reliefs also opened up a magic means of flight. A mysterious warmth and organic unity made him different from other Constructivists.

The modern house reminds us more and more of a UFO: we cannot avoid the flight; it is imminent.

We are surrounded by an extraordinarily immeasurable and crazy world and we try to reflect on its mysterious sounds in our buildings. What is going on in Estonia at the moment could be taken as a huge performance. We can only guess at the outlines of the future. Matter seeks a new form for itself every day, constantly improving its structure; we can suppose that the object will soon be ready. Perhaps it resembles a dark piano, smashed to pieces against a white background, where magical black images form a chaotic new relationship.

There is a proud feeling in the air of freedom, of initiative in art and of being different. For an architect, it is a dangerous but highly promising time. He may get lost, he may drown in the general turmoil, but at the same time new relations and elements, new people, opportunities, ways and bridges are opening up for us. The sculptor has fresh materials from which to create form. The old Constructivist slogan 'Art organises life' is turned upside-down, and now life in artists' hands becomes something different. The new kinetic sculpture begins to move in a different way. Man's own depth is as immeasurable as the possibilities in art are infinite.

Ich, das wissenschaftliche und kalte Erkennen der Wirklichkeit, gleichsam ein Vorwärtsschreiten über die Stufen einer unendenden Treppe, so erinnert das Unermeßliche Erkennen an ein unendliches System, wirklich vollendeter in sich ge- schlossener Sphären!

## guy Lafranchi

### Archonpoison

Archonpoison design drawing

... If you are willing to accept all of the premises operating in the development of cities, you do not need theory because it has been given to you. But if you say that I cannot accept all of these assumptions or I do not want to operate within them, you are obliged to develop your own theory ...
— Lebbeus Woods

Archonpoison deals with structures that are welcome or not, forgotten, destroyed or 'nicely' renovated, accepted or despised. On the surface, these all look forward to the activation of their own transformation, neither to be replaced, nor to end up in archives of conservation. They transform poison power. In history, new creative impulses have often emerged from wounded or decaying environments, political disasters, natural catastrophes, etc.: cultural growth on poisoned ground.

Examples could range from a system of empty oil and petrol storage tanks close to Bern, to a historical building such as the so-called 'Bernese Landhaus'. The latter is regarded as poison because of its social isolation and the inherent absence of communication both in the house and in its surroundings. What these examples have in common is something added to the existing structure to provoke activation and transformation. For instance, the fuel in the system of connecting pipes is no longer petrol, but information. The pipes become data-highways. Independent levels of science, culture etc., nest in the tank system and begin to communicate. Exchange and decentralisation of knowledge result – dynamic individual perception. The aim is a symbiosis of technological mass activation and the individual experimentation field.

I am interested in edge conditions, produced by the physical/conceptual definitions that offer a field of movement, independent of scale. We see more and more virtual reality: architecture is becoming an escape from reality. Within this edge condition, reality could/should be brought back into built space.

Archonpoison is a thought-model that is not to be compared with the thinking processes of so-called collective consciousness. It is not influenced by a media-driven collective concept of aesthetics.

When 'contextualism' and 'typological historicism' are no more than a set of disguises applied to oven-ready formulae, how can architecture be a means by which society discovers new territories or knowledge?

Visual-tactile, syntax-mosaic, mechanical-organic, sequence-simultaneity, composition-improvisation, continuous-discontinuous – the space between these expressions is the area of movement.

The economy, politics and other prevailing institutions are put into question. Free individuals open to experimentation are invited. Fine, but how do we proceed from the present disaster to this world of dreams? This borderline interests me: the transition of systems, or how activation takes place; transition from linear connections into the world of creative configurations; the hybrid principle as a technique of creative discovery. The meeting of two media is a moment of truth and revelation from which new form is born. As we know, people are not yet willing to experiment; uncertainties are dispelled as soon as possible.

Projection screens, auditoria, linking of tanks to each other and connection to global networks, experimentation chambers, availability of freely selectable information levels – the principle is of an implosive mosaic, characteristic of all levels of electronic data transfer.

A kind of self regulation is made possible by the fact that open architecture makes corrections and spontaneous combinations possible. It has to do with the non-linearity of network patterns. It extends in all directions.

The design process does not stop at the building permit but is extended into production. One task for me as an architect is to touch upon things that help others (of any profession) to go to the next step of their own discipline. Therefore a field of decision-making, imagination and innovation has to be left open in order to activate the power of unpredictability, of experimentation.

# Lars Lerup

Weather and Household Vehicles, Houston

Table

The sky is a huge bag of air, articulated by aeroplanes, helicopters and the grandiose machinations of weather which roll into the upper strata either quietly or with terrifying fanfare. Shaped like whacked-out species from an exotic aquarium – huge partially disintegrated flounders, schools of drunken piranhas, bloated whales – slow, fast, frazzled, mostly opaque, and surrounded by wisps of indecisive greyish-brown mists, clouds often operate in opposite directions. Entire seasons pass in minutes, raising or dropping the temperature, making the surprised and innocent drifters under the canopy change their clothes like models working the catwalk. Thunder is poised to deliver, and flashes draw the most random connections: cloud to cloud, cloud to building, cloud to ground. Independent along the horizon, hideous verticals etch cracks in the black heavens, foretelling human disaster. Or rain totally ignores gravity by operating in every conceivable direction: up, down, sideways, towards you, and away from you, sucking you into its destiny; nature rampant. Unlike the lower strata, this huge stadium seems underdeveloped begging for more towers, more air traffic, more lights – introduced, if for nothing else, to counteract the forces of nature, to challenge its total dominance. As it stands now, nature shares equal ground with artifice, while the bag of air above would rule – if it were not for pollution.

Brown fumes, fiery sunsets – pollution fills the days when the weather rests. The yellow, static girdle of haze binds together the sky and the ground. Creating a third ecology, the vapour drops invisibly through the canopy of trees to slip into the drifters' nostrils, lungs and eyes. Sinus capital of the world. Yet it is only above the canopy with the benefit of foreshortening that pollution builds its body, and makes its demanding presence visible. An immense, unwanted backlash, the pollution-as-surplus reminds us of the price of our mobility.

Essay by Neil Spiller

'Mechanization' endows inanimate matter with the properties of gesture. Every movement is meaningful because its intended object, the product, is shaped or formed by it. Its being manufactured communicates an intention of its maker that centres on knowing and being in the world. A product invariably recalls the move-ments of the hand or machine that 'gestured' it into existence.

WOR(L)DS OF DANIEL LIBESKIND, Raoul Bunschoten, AA FILES No. 10

The early theoretical works of Daniel Libeskind are often denounced as scribble, whether it is the THEATRUM MUNDI or the precise inscriptions of CHAMBER WORKS. But this is a fool's analysis. These, and many of Libeskind's writings, seek to reveal and articulate a search for architecture's *prima materia*: the elusive relationship between made and maker in a world in which architecture cannot even rely on the old geometries of Plato, Euclid and Descartes; a world where fields of gravity, of symbol and orthogonality have been smashed for ever.

Even the felicity of the drawing is broken because its status is forever being reassessed and re-presented. Such early, seminal works define an architectural space that speaks of enigma, of chance, of almost cabalistic geometries with oblique nuances. They strip aside the certainties and ascribed values of the architectural object and the ill-fitting coat of skins with which sophism has clothed it. These works have no truck with the guilt associated with architectural production and its urge to make sense to a variety of untutored eyes. The work places itself outside the immediate ownership of the viewer who, like the Beasty Boys, has 'to fight for the right to party' in its contorted spaces. There are no clues in these striated spaces.

Libeskind seems to be at his best when exploring the theme of death, whether the demise of architecture or the genocide of the Holocaust. His work itself is tortured, broken and fragmented, sliced and gouged. But these cuts and surgical incisions are not malevolent. He uses the instrument of pain to create closure and healing. This is certainly true in his iconic Jewish Museum in Berlin, arguably the most interesting building constructed in the last half of the twentieth century. Here, Libeskind evokes perhaps the most unfashionable aspect of late-twentieth-century architectural practice: symbolism. He recoats it,

recasts it and hollows out its insides. Using this tactic, he creates an architecture that plays on the symbolic language of absence, the much-discussed void at the centre of his work and at the centre of the Jewish soul. Here is an architect whose language is that of yearning, distress, angst and terrible fear; yet he has enough control of his art still to posit an architecture of hope.

Like his buildings, his texts are prized as intelligent enigmas; as much for what isn't there as for what is.

Libeskind's extension for the Victoria & Albert Museum in London gives the capital an opportunity to gain a building of real international stature and to abandon its fixation with the diluted 'hi-tech' style now regularly debased by all and sundry. Its fractal cladding is perhaps an indication of Libeskind's fascination with the ascalar qualities of architectural space and form. Those qualities are aptly illustrated in his well-known theoretical work, MICROMEGAS. Here, he creates dense perspectival intensities or fields, whose formal qualities recede into the distance without losing their formal articulation or familial affiliations.

Libeskind is also an inspiring teacher, and has nurtured some of architecture's most original and, one must say, way-out, theorists. These include Jesse Reiser, Ben Nicholson, Raoul Bunschoten and Don Bates, all of whom have gone on to leave marks on the contemporary scene, and some of whom are in this book.

After the vagaries of Modernism it is through Libeskind that many place their faith in modern architecture. Here at last is an architect whose language is not only equal to the thorny question of remembrance, but is also equal to that of chance and its sometimes malevolent and terrible

Extension to Victoria and Albert
Museum, London, 1998 (top)
Jewish Museum, Berlin, 1998 (bottom)

power, its fearful oppressions and dangers and to the brighter sides of architectural aspiration; a light in the blackness, so to speak.

Libeskind pushes the simple-minded issues extant in architectural composition through its fractal roof. His architecture speaks of more than the inane particulars of building materials and their methods of junctioning. He understands that it is posited, articulated and sited in an infinity of spatial, phenomenological and psychological fields, each capable of distorting or embellishing the reading of his work. His is not an architecture that is aesthetically or emotionally safe. If balance is what you seek, do not enter the labyrinth of Libeskind.

The role of the square and courtyard, crucial to the urban context of the Bloomsbury area, is spatially reversed. The positive space has been fractured and sculpted into an internal courtyard housing the exhibition spaces, an inhabitable void, enclosed within four kinetic walls.

The blank south elevation of the Bloomsbury Theatre bounds the site to the north. The scale and presence of the wall has been utilised to maximum effect as a 'screen', coated in photo-reflective paint, on which to cast shadows and shafts of light. The southern boundary of the site is formed by the end wall of the Victorian terrace. Light is projected through the building on to the wall, signposting the collections on each floor. The west wall of the building forms the Temporary Display area for the Slade Collection of contemporary art, split over two floors.

A folded copper envelope encloses approximately one-third of the building. In plan the building is 'U'-shaped, with the base at the west end. Embedded and folded into the copper is a deep 'ravine' housing a staircase from ground level to the roof-top restaurant. The depth of the ravine varies, allowing the 'climber' occasional select views. The copper walls wrap around the front elevation, isolating some exhibition spaces from natural light and allowing the temperature and humidity to be controlled accurately. This creates a vertical court (20 metres tall) between the wall and the glazed 'Interactive Facade' on Gordon Street to the east.

The facade is punctured twice to provide public access. Running the full height of the building, it is arranged in a vertical pattern of small panes. The outer layer is laminated glass, and the internal is liquid-crystal laminate, which is transparent only when an electrical current is passed through it via switches located in the floors of the main staircase and the information-technology balconies. When a movement triggers a switch, the glass becomes clear for as long as the switch is activated. The facade is constantly in a transient state.

The entrance is formed by a narrow vertical fissure in the copper shroud. A glass tunnel travels deep into the building, providing a view up into the exhibition spaces and overlooking the Petrie Collection below. The route forms a link between Gordon Square and the University College south cloisters and contrasts with the vehicle access ramp, which penetrates the building in a concrete tunnel.

Deep spaces and offset decks are evident on the internal route to the top. At entry level the internal courtyard is mainly horizontal but begins to fracture over the lecture hall. The staircase widens in the open space, sharpening as it doubles back to climb to the next deck. Cutting in and out of the exhibition decks, the route gives access to observation points, deep vertical views and display areas. The cargo lift and glazed passenger lift to the restaurant serve as fixed co-ordinates for the twisting journey. Popping out of the copper shroud into the restaurant, the visitor is presented with an unrestricted view of west London. The glazed south panels can be swung up to create a contrast with the internal, confined exhibition spaces.

The Strang Collection is sandwiched between the Slade spaces. Study tables and display cabinets occupy the majority of the floor area. There is also an 'extended gallery' on the virtual reality balcony. The Petrie Collection is housed on the bottom floor, 10 metres below the lobby, from where the larger exhibits can be viewed. Descent is required to the stepped basement for closer inspection. The Flexible Exhibition Space has a 6-metre floor-to-ceiling clearance.

At night, light can be seen to seep and leak from the museum, highlighting the cracks and fissures in the skin, and the restaurant appears to float on top of the building. Light issuing from the exhibition spaces spills on to the shadow wall.

Undisplayed works are housed in storage towers, which penetrate the floor decks creating vertical shafts connecting all levels. Light and humidity are kept under strict control. Images of all the works will be transferred to computer and can be examined on the virtual reality balconies. An accurate record can be kept and viewing restrictions can be imposed for the more fragile pieces in the collection.

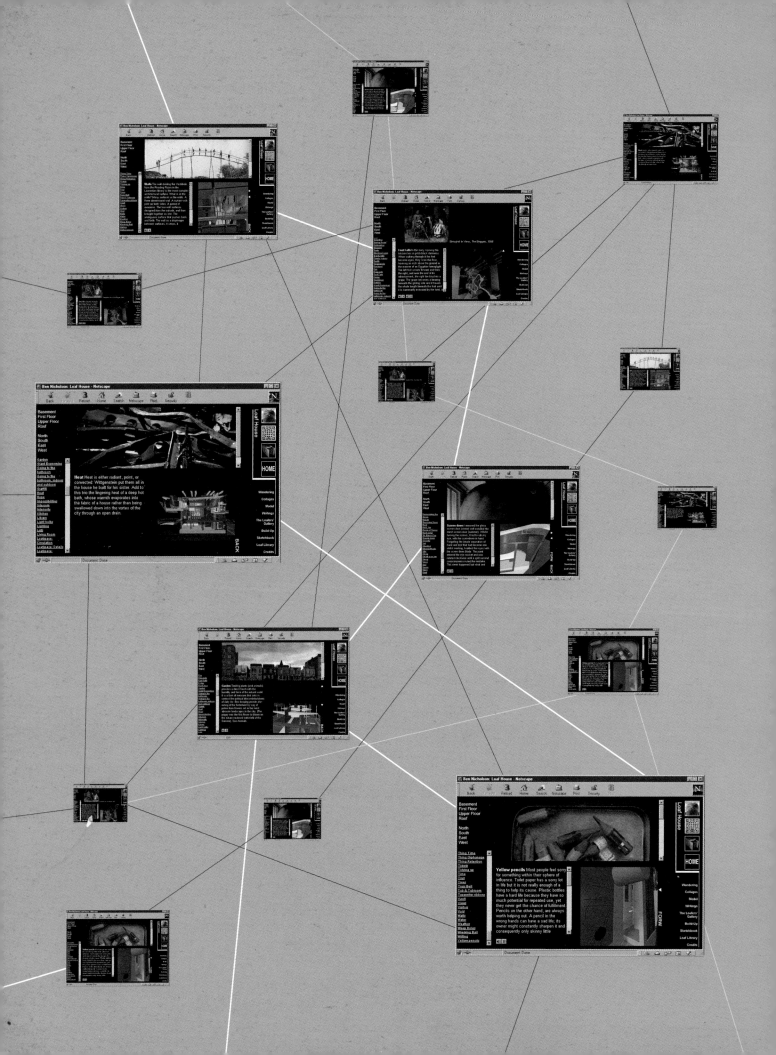

ben nicholson

Click It. Click It Good.

Loaf House

Envisage a place that could reflect every facet of cultural achievement; a place that includes everything ever done, being done, and planned for the future. By leaning into this imaginary space, the hunger of being human could be satiated. 'Architecture' (a wholly abstract word used to define a collective entity) is at present best manifested by the making of a building. A building takes in every endeavour of humanity – be it law, history, ethics, the spirit, the elements, management of money, politics, people, art or science. The great works of architecture go part way to meet these impossible ideals, finding a method to pull together the library-like nature of humanity. The Greek temple builders or the medieval cathedral makers were able to forge a thing that was all-inclusive, making a singular object capable of touching every corner of the psyche, inside and out, and in the process creating a massive n-dimensional vision of the world, perhaps an early version of a whopping great big world-wide website.

Enter, on cue, the World Wide Web: the encyclopedic space that would find the trappings of built fabric stifling and archaic. It is no coincidence that today's information organisers unabashedly hand out business cards printed with the word 'Architect' to define their profession. For them, this word says it all: a way of thought that is truly accessible and pleasurable. They make and organise space that anyone can enter and get a buzz from. Theirs is a place where time forward, backward and time around are given value. They have the tools that make the profession of builder seem inadequate and pedantic.

After hitting the Web, experiencing architecture is never quite the same. A visit to a Gothic cathedral takes on the guise of logging on to a brilliantly organised website. The cursor has retrained the eye to glide over the surface of the building. The three entrance portals are surveyed and one is clicked to gain access to somewhere new. On passing through the portal, the eye again clicks on a sculpture to know more about its face, and inside the cavernous void of the cathedral the mind darts about, clicking on everything, both objects and ambience. The hyper-visitor has just crashed architecture's party, to un-tech the well-manicured, encyclopedic nature of experience.

For those used to clicking in the public realm, some architectural spaces are better than others. A seasoned clicker goes berserk in a six-teenth-century *studiolo*, a tiny room favoured by Italian dukes, in which their whole being is described in wood intarsia by a cross-reference of figures, stabilised by perspectival building-scapes. Wherever the eye roams there is something to see.

A clicker's worst nightmare is Modernist buildings devoid of compound clues about the intricacies of human endeavour. The Modernists posited the notion that only singular examples of phenomena are required to represent related experience. A glass vase with a few blooms is enough to signify nature, four walls symbolise the history of containment, and a hovering flat roof is adequate to keep the weather mute – Modernism's biggest mistake by far and proof of its hubris. Elemental reduction and the intolerant striving for purity are too much for humanity to bear, for simplification gives too few clues to stimulate the intricacies of life. Today's Formic Blobists, who have attached themselves to Modernism's coat tails, can do little to right this imbalance. Fearful of hypertext's mercurial black water, they resort to the electric frieze, displaying menus of discarded emotions, to fix the problem.

The clicker, a spatial guerrilla, has invented a new realm that is alert and receptive to a different sort of beauty from the one we have held dear for decades. When a clicker visits the Parthenon Elgin's Marbles are cut from London and effortlessly pasted to Athens; and should a story of each stone figure be called for, its frame will be clicked for content. In 1911, when the world witnessed Picasso's Cubist paintings, it could not go back to what it used to know. Today, clickers experience the same predicament, only this time the necessity for the builder's trowel to be the sole renderer of architectural space is being outstared, and someone's about to blink.

79

# Kyong park

Images of the Future and
the Architecture of a New Geography

Petroli Towers, Kuala Lumpur

Cities are sites of violence. We keep on simultaneously building and destroying them. These endless cycles of destruction and construction may be intrinsic to the progress of the urban environment, yet their excessive recurrence seems beyond the adaptive limit of inhabitants. One could envisage a future where modernity, ruthless in the use of natural resources and human labour, may leave a trail of abandoned cities lying exhausted along the route of advancing capitalism.

In truth, however, cities are just moving, shifting their boundaries across the land. Enclosure no longer protects communities, it destroys them. At the same time as the density of suburbs begins to exceed that of the inner cities – in developed nations at least – the enclosure now protects the periphery rather than the centre. The concept of enclosure, the very principle on which cities were founded, is in transformation.

And, within the standardised geography of 'everywhere but nowhere', both the centre and the edges of any city or culture seem superfluous. With generic malls, hotels and offices now dominating skylines and public spaces, the homogenisation of urban identity is integral to the internationalisation of labour, commerce and information. The goal is the convenience of having cities that look and feel the same; that conform to the standards and comforts expected by increasingly globalised industries and their professionals. And in binding distinctive and distant landscapes, the architecture of globalisation constructs an immaterial city, one that is lacking a particular location but is nevertheless quite real and functional.

In order to achieve the franchising of urban and cultural spaces, the history of any particular place must be modified, and in some cases, eradicated outright. For example, many Asian cities, amid urban developments of monumental proportions, are erasing their traditional sectors and building standardised urban and cultural landscapes, all Western inspired. In turn, the remnants of indigenous architecture and spaces, now dysfunctional in both economic and cultural terms, could only survive through their thematisation as restaurants, museums and amusement parks. With the absence of 'active' culture, selected memories are being reconstituted as 'official' history, and returned to the urban fabric, stripped of their precision and idiosyncracies and primarily attached to massive commercialised spaces. As much as the Asian officials claim that the Westernisation of

their cities is not literal but interpretive, the survival of traditional ways of life will be virtually impossible without their icons and symbols.

And with the Western colonisation of Asia reaching its closing chapter, as exemplified by the recent transfer of Hong Kong from British rule to Chinese control, the power of colonialism is shifting. Although the general transformation of urban landscape, from indigenous to Western, was brought about in the interest of foreign investment and trade, the foreigners now lament the loss of native cultures more than the natives. Post-colonialism induces voluntary self-exploitation of natural and human resources. In this condition of self-colonisation, the eradication of native culture may be more ruthless under the natives than under the foreigners because the transformation of the built environment confronts less resistance.

In contrast, the dissolution of the Cold War has invoked a resurgence of national, regional and local identities. Wars in Korea, Vietnam and Afghanistan are replaced by conflicts in Iraq, Somalia, Chechnya, Zaire, Rwanda and elsewhere as the geopolitical landscape is reconstituted into regional, urban and even neighbourhood-scale divisions. And although many neo-nationalist groups may have been provoked by self-serving political and financial ambitions, the new mapping nevertheless seems quintessential to the self-identity of indigenous masses. For them, revolution is spatial, and their battles are over spaces and buildings.

Thus cities, no longer targeted by atomic weapons, now implode from their own disappointments and developments. Different sets of urban issues, of political dominance and social oppression, are being brought forth, accompanied by

pictures of burning buildings and exploded public spaces—in the World Trade Center, Oklahoma City, Sarajevo, Beirut and elsewhere. The movements for independence are now emerging even within the 'First World', not just in some 'banana republics'. With the internalisation of political debates and popular dissent, architecture becomes the new political effigy, and cities the immersive theatres of economic, political and cultural conflagrations. If these are the images of our future, then they must be the architecture of a new social geography in the making.

In the end, we seem to be making many nations out of one city, and at the same time, making one city from many nations. The desire to be international at any cost, combined with the renewed emphasis on local identity, is producing a phenomenon of 'glocalisation' – a diabolical mix of universalism and individualism. In the attempt to reconcile this contradiction, old boundaries are being broken and new maps are being drawn, radically mutating our social and individual spaces.

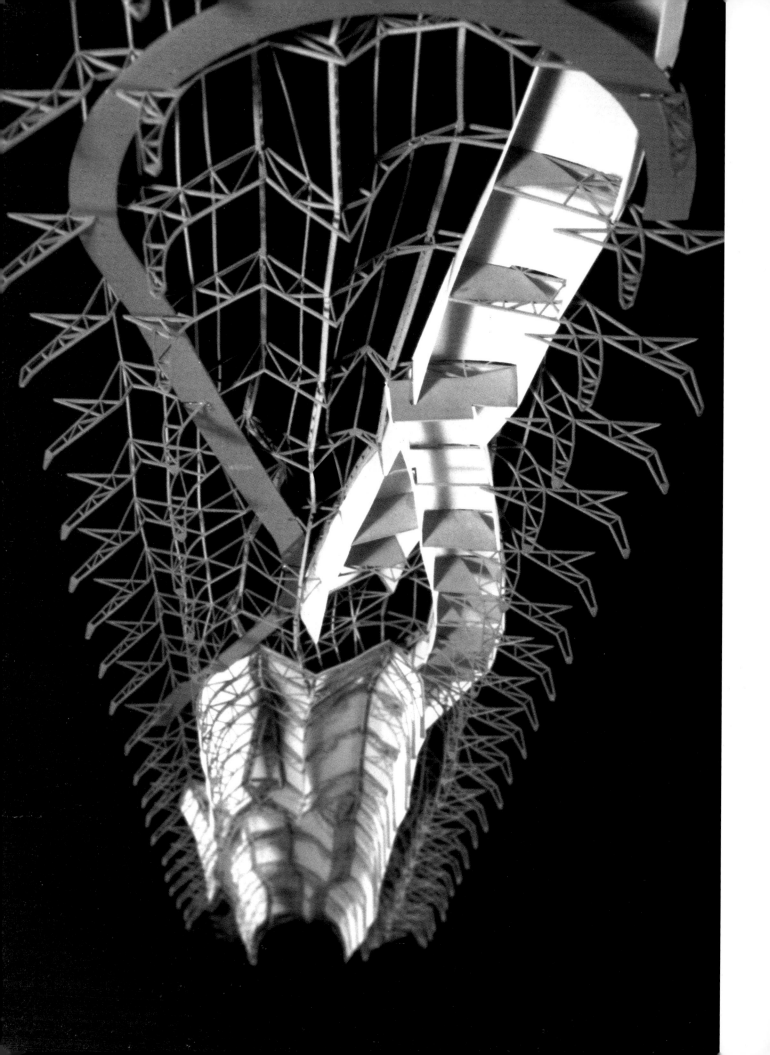

Essay by Neil Spiller

In a 'supple' employment of geodetics one finds many properties and possibilities. Historically and operationally, geodetics falls between two totalising systems, the skeletal model and the structural skin, as in monocoque construction. On a possible expanded reading, however, geodetics act as structural tissue or flesh – an intermediate structure that could assemble heterogeneous agglomerations of space, programme and path. Moreover, geodetics is protean in the sense that the structure has the capability of changing and adapting to the space that it developed in a number of ways: by changing the fineness or coarseness of its reticulations; by growing or multiplying the number of struts or crossovers; by mimicking the surfaces of conventional structure upon which it is projected; or by changing by degrees the type of infill or skin it carries.
—Jesse Reiser 'Some notes on Geodetics' SITES AND STATIONS – PROVISIONAL UTOPIAS edited by Stan Allen with Kyong Park Lusitania Press (New York) 1995 p.207

Reiser + Umemoto are masters of the fold, the curve and the geodetic structure – a web of delicate beams, akin to a fishnet stocking. Used in many of the great World War II bombers, these geodetic webs are fields that conjoin, stretch and squish together in response to fluctuations in programme, ground condition and traffic-flow factors, which are amongst a whole array of dynamic forces that push and pull their structures this way and that. This practice rejoices in the disjuncture between global transport systems and their infrastructure, and local site conditions. It is from this initial, awkward juxtaposition that the strategy for architectural resolution begins to take shape, aided by the inherent flexibility of the geodetic skin.

A new form of public space arises out of the interaction of two logics: first, the close proximity of major institutions and corporations; and second, a consequent influx of smaller institutions and services that are sustained by the presence of their larger institutions. The success of such co-dependent organisations is predicated not simply on the major institutions that initiate the information zone, but on their capacity to act as catalysts for the advent of new programmes and uses.
The proposal for the Kansai Library thus embodies two distinct yet related imperatives: to fulfil the explicit programmatic criteria of the library while developing implicit spatialities that would foster the new and unforeseen irruptions of programme brought about by the information zone.
—Jesse Reiser, 'Kansai Kan of the National Diet Library, Kansai, Japan' AD 'ARCHITECTURE AFTER GEOMETRY' PROFILE No.127 edited by Peter Davidson & Donald L. Bates 1996 p.93

Reiser + Umemoto's competition entry for the Yokohama International Port Terminal also echoes these preoccupations. It is a massive shed, 412 metres long, with spans of 42.5 metres. Yet it is a highly articulated shed – a shed with a difference:

The structure springs from hinges placed at the surface of the main level. These are carried on concrete piers extending from the basement parking level through the apron to the surface of the main level. Horizontal thrust from the arches is counteracted by tension rods connecting opposing arch hinges. These tension rods also serve as partial support for the main floor slab. This large shed, though affiliated with its nineteenth-century antecedents, differs in the sense that while the latter were characterised by a totalising conception employing uniform and repetitive structural units enclosing a

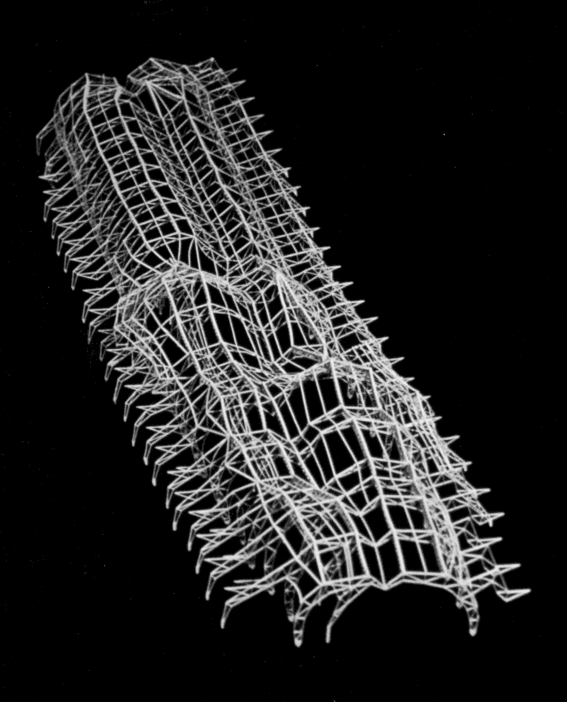

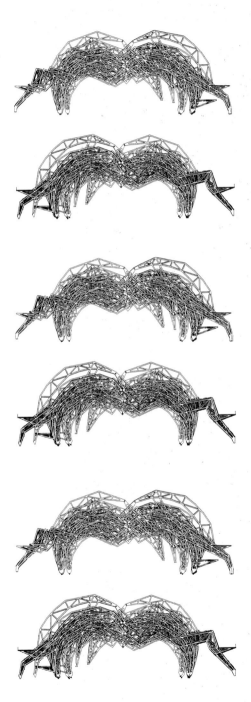

single homogeneous space, this proposal engenders hetererogeneity through selective perturbations and extensions of the structural frames. This transformation yields a complex of spaces smoothly incorporating the multiple terminal, civic, and garden programmes within and below its span.

The structure seems to hug the ground, appearing to produce a new, yet contextual, artificial surface: at once alien and peculiar to its setting. To achieve such beautiful interventions requires a remarkable skill in programme manipulation and creative juxtaposition. The Yokohama Terminal would not be complete without a ship in port, docked to its outreaching arms.

Reiser + Umemoto's work is identified by the fluidity of their structural propositions. It is not about the self-contained, pristine object but about the need to mesh into the context, to complete their surroundings without remaining exclusive. It never denies the unexpected creative opportunities of alien occupation.

The geometry of our urban infrastructure, its information highways and ever more complex use patterns demand architectures that can alter and change. These non-linear geometries have superseded the rational and the orthogonal. Reiser + Umemoto's practice is constantly researching such contextual dynamics.

# Kevin rhowbotham

## From Object to Landscape

Field drawing, territory series;
No. 0710; perspective

What amuses me or, more precisely, goads me, is that suddenly, and from nowhere, as if by some spontaneous, hidden, telluric mechanism, a change of considerable dimensions has insinuated itself within the consciousness of architects. At least this is how social appearance has it; most certainly from the vertiginous vantage point of the so-called critical edge. Where there once was object, now there is landscape. A style is born.

Some advice: to this malediction of objectness, this designed tumescence of matter, apply an analgesic: aspirin by mouth. I knew a woman, by unfortunate association, who suffered so severely from migraine that on the sudden and general availability of aspirin, which abruptly cured her complaint, named her daughter 'Aspirina', so conjoining, by conceptual inference and historical fact, her head with her vagina.

Would that architects were so conceptual they might, with blind magnanimity, conceive an affective association between body and world that becomes as spiritual as this. As psychological, as viscerally direct, as an act of love.

Some more advice: 'There are acts of love and extravagant magnanimity after which nothing is more advisable than to take a stick and give the eyewitness a thrashing and so confuse his memory': Frederick Nietzsche, BEYOND GOOD AND EVIL.

From the critical edge – for architecture this amounts to a precipitous but hardly elevated position – and following a concerted unconscious retrenchment against the object as the fulcrum of a Formalist discourse, there now emanates a new but equally disingenuous *cri de coeur*, to wit: let there be topography – as if breasts were not enough.

The protuberant, unyielding hardness of the object, boyishly virile, even priapic in its pompous mechanical attitude, has been contested by a certain formal flaccidity and organic vagination. The object: one could almost personify it as the chin of Arnold Schwarzenegger, the mannered submission of Madonna; could its image finally be vacillating?

Will architecture's mechanistic ideological metaphor suffer a structural revision; from cock to bunny, from hard to soft, from object to landscape? After landscape, surely softness is a key term, to the extent that these days every dreary nuance that grovels after notoriety seems to append it, signifying, not least for my own perverse sensibility, a talismanic shift into the codex of visceral and vaginal interiority from the vantage of mass culture, albeit dead on arrival; hence soft-house, soft-box, soft-ware, soft-lad, soft-ball, soft-pop, soft-money, soft-net, soft-sex, soft-sell, soft-scape, soft-space.

Further advice: sophistication, I seem to recall, signifies a contrived adulteration in the manner of abstruse sophist circumlocution; precisely, cant, as the Oxbridgians like to call bullshit.

Soft-topography is the contrived result; the lewd association of a torso with a computer on a drafting table. And we, the circumnavigated, are invited to confide in it as a new style of architecture, in strict commodity fashion.

If architecture were a woman, as Nietzsche might have it, then she would be, firstly, penetrable; but only in appearance. She would be political because this is the means to power in complicity. She would, to the eye at least, be soft. She would be interior. She would be – and this is her most horrific and evil attribute – persuasive rather than declarative. By making the body a machine, a wat-ery limpidity is avoided. Brutalised fact builds the houses of our consciousness from the outside: always from the outside.

And you my dear reader, please consider this seriously. If, like the mother of Aspirina, your taste is for direct action, then think from the inside; from the womb. In this culture, amneoscenticity is interred in concrete. Alienation is the mass result.

A warning: 'Specialists without spirit, sensualists without heart; this nullity imagines that it has attained a level of civilisation never before achieved.' Max Weber, ASCETICISM AND THE SPIRIT OF CAPITALISM. I despair of course, but out of sight – the only sane condition for a sensitive man.

Another warning: the symphony in which convulsive self-importance sets the meter for an

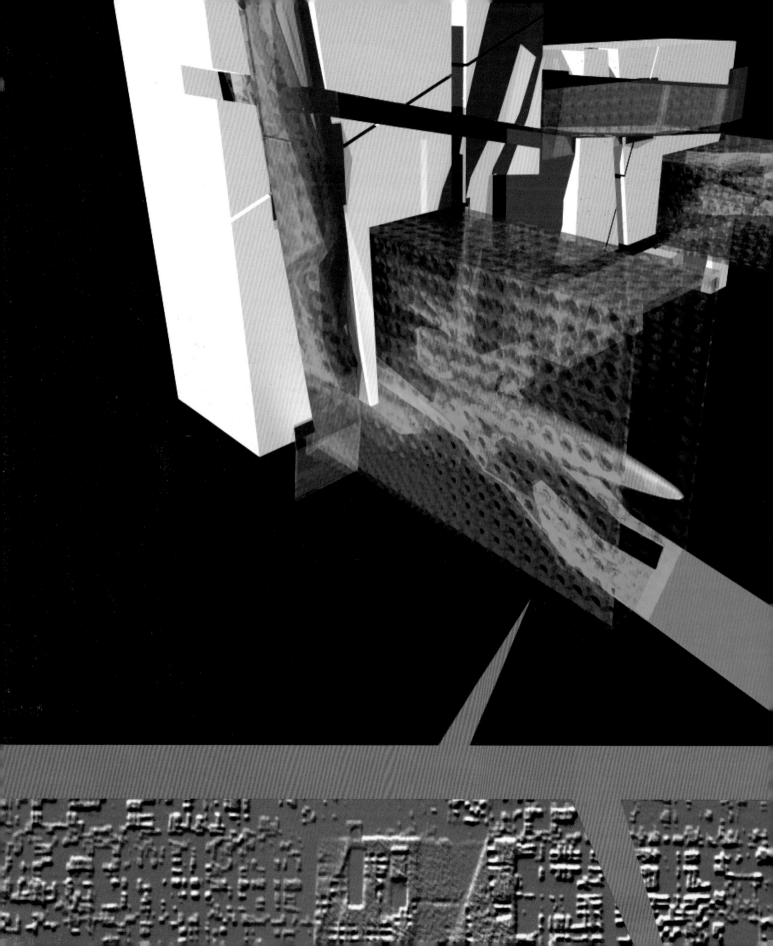

endemic structural corruption presses self-
censorship to play the adagio.

Let me invite you to think the following: beyond
the object is the landscape, at an angle. Only the
rabid Cartesian angularities of architecture can
conceive of a flat earth after Copernicus. But tell
me, don't you notice that the city seems to be a
kind of cutting, at intervals of 5 metres or so? An
empty bookcase between mammarial hills. Surely
this is a perversion.

Or are you thinking right now, that such a spec-
ulation, concerning things visceral, concerning
things of the very gut, has no legitimate, not to say,
tasteful position within your hot-washed and
desiccated cosmology? So much the worse for
you. You are already glacial, like the architectures
of the Net, whatever they might be. Glacial, frozen
smooth, impenetrable, transparent, revealing all,
in the sense of Zamyatin's city of numbers; a truly
anomic desert of a place. But let's not kid ourselves: this is the very image that drives out
fulminating desire; liquid sensuality. A flat scape
is a power space; an ascetic lifebelt of sorts
around your venal genitalia, which saves your
head for dry things by keeping your crotch above
the fluid.

In order to describe the work of Helmut Richter and a handful of other international architects with similar concerns, a new term is required in place of the overused 'hi-tech'. Something like 'hand-tailored tech' would better represent this particular critical seam in mid-to-late twentieth-century architecture.

The atmosphere of the architecture school at Graz in the 1960s can be imagined. Somehow detached from the main traffic of Europe and implicitly critical towards Vienna and the self-consciousness of its high culture, it had its own inventive approach and a quizzical set of professors who could escape the endless bitching of the big city. Its students created a disproportionate number of strange machines and original combinations of hardware, not all deriving from buildings *per se*, and almost always using working parts. Richter's graduating thesis already reflected what was to be the most elegant and considered end of this output. In fact it is so strong that in 1998 he relaunched a part of it in a successful competition scheme for bank-cafés.

Richter's postgraduate studies were undertaken at UCLA, an institution that has certain parallels with Graz. Away from the ever-critical and culturally self-conscious East Coast, the department of architecture had been infiltrated by Archigram, Reyner Banham and Arata Isozaki. The inherited culture was via Schindler, Neutra, Eames, Craig Ellwood and Konrad Wachsmann (who was still playing with his universal-joint machine down the street at USC). Richter's friendship with the young English group, Chrysalis, led to his sharing a house with them in Paris when they followed Piano and Rogers to build the Pompidou Centre.

Thus we can log a period of some nine or ten years of sustained conversation in which design was certainly not about following the well-behaved rules of Formalism or Rationalism but to do with new ideas and inventions. The manners displayed by the parts of his buildings recall those inherent Austrian niceties, such as the jewel-like fashioning of corners, joints and edges, only when they need to. His work is less fussy than that of many of his friends, its occasional sumptuousness being found in line.

Perhaps the chosen cities of his development were even subconsciously anticipated, for his student work contained small designed objects that could easily have occupied certain corners of Chareau's glass house, and moving parts that might well have responded to Wachsmann's universal joint; and the later, larger buildings certainly have the directness of the best American work.

The most studied parts of Richter's output have something more, however, than neat and witty combinations of metal, glass and plastic. There is a special lyricism of line and a delight in absorbing the critical joint or an interleaving of sheets that recalls the work of Eileen Gray or of the Asplund-Jakobsen-Aalto syndrome. Unlike his English friends, he has pursued an architecture of very clear and direct concepts through what I like to think of as the 'Richter Relaxed Detail'.

In his early Chinese Restaurant, 'Kwang', the skinned rear wall is as deceptively simple as the flap of a tent. For his social housing in southern Vienna, the public space is separated from the street by a tantalisingly subtle series of faceted glass – of considerable size – held by the most simple bolting system. The facets are separated not by complicated slivers of skin, but by air: the surfaces are free-standing, avoiding an expensive and fussy set of details. Similarly replete with such confident, simple solutions are the Vienna school and the Japanese restaurant in the 3rd district of Vienna. Yet Richter is no mere miniaturist: the school in particular asserts itself as a total, immediately readable figure, with enormous grids of glass that expose major spaces within a series of planes, only to complete their encompassment with a couple of lyrical staircases (which carry the conversation started by Gropius and Meyers' Faguswerke stair into the late twentieth century).

At this moment, however, his response to the tricky and often frustrating tradition of public housing is the most impressive part of the work.

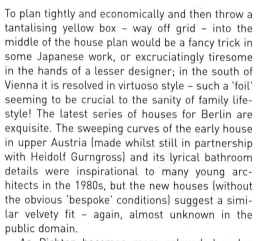

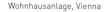
Wohnhausanlage, Vienna

To plan tightly and economically and then throw a tantalising yellow box – way off grid – into the middle of the house plan would be a fancy trick in some Japanese work, or excruciatingly tiresome in the hands of a lesser designer; in the south of Vienna it is resolved in virtuoso style – such a 'foil' seeming to be crucial to the sanity of family life-style! The latest series of houses for Berlin are exquisite. The sweeping curves of the early house in upper Austria (made whilst still in partnership with Heidolf Gurngross) and its lyrical bathroom details were inspirational to many young arc-hitects in the 1980s, but the new houses (without the obvious 'bespoke' conditions) suggest a simi-lar velvety fit – again, almost unknown in the public domain.

As Richter becomes more relaxed, he also becomes more refined – a unique trajectory.

Essay by Peter Cook

J Walter Thompson Headquarters,
Frankfurt, 1996

Till Schneider and Michael Schumacher practise in Frankfurt, build in Berlin, Leipzig and Frankfurt and have their antennae out into the web of Europe. The most immediate quality of their work is its true mixture of finesse and clarity, both tactile and conceptual and applying equally to total image and the playing out of parts. A tricky commodity in the current architectural world, 'clarity' often turns out to be dullness masquerading as simplicity.

Already completed are the Red Pavilion in Berlin and the J Walter Thompson Headquarters in Frankfurt. The clarity of the former, a red box, is accentuated by the fact that it is poised upon naughty legs. Such legs would not, of course, have been considered naughty at all in the Rio of the 1950s, only in these more puritanical times. They are fine-tuned however, in a way that would not have been expected in the 1950s, and the intervals of glass positioned within the redness of the box occur with a sobering degree of inevitability. In the abstract, the juxtaposition of humour and seriousness and the flag-like redness sounds erotic or exotic. In fact, the box succeeds in its role as an icon in a city already full of icons, and as a question-mark to those many older and worthier names who seem to build their most unsure pieces in Berlin.

The red box represents a seminal piece of decision-making. Like the London birdcage of Price–Snowdon–Newby or the Santa Monica Place of Gehry, the building knows its moment. All these constructions contain a single and obvious proposition, held within a shell and armature and that merit constant reinspection. Such predictable elements as stair-cases or openings become delightful.

In the Frankfurt building there is a parallel clarity. A heroic space lies outside the 'crate' of offices, ready to absorb the poetry of the diagonal stair route and a series of balconies. Nearly gratuitous, these are atmospherically and tectonically succinct, providing a place where an employee can step out for a cigarette, a quiet chat, or a breath of the fresh air that is subtly drawn up through this zone of the building.

The inside-outside space has been so clearly and finely drawn that it would seem to have come from the hands of a more experienced or larger office, its assurance enabling a succinct organisational statement to be followed up by a lucid definition of parts and planes. Thus the fine edge, the cool division, the well-proportioned leg, plate, base, cut are always evident.

I knew Schneider and Schumacher as postgraduate students at the Staedelschule in Frankfurt, each producing a project that remains a seminal piece in the development of that extraordinary little hothouse. Schneider's twisting office block took an audacious geometrical proposition far beyond the predictable limits of 'what to do with an interesting shape', giving it a true spatial quality. Schumacher's 'digger' for Kassel evacuated space and then, at a certain stage, became itself a heroic piece of industrial archaeology that was simultaneously a working circulation system. So I have followed with interest these particular talents – their dexterity and discrimination as well as their ability to wheedle more out of a piece of envelope than most of us would imagine possible. The power of this controlled architecture is in its imploded formalism.

Schneider and Schumacher fully understand light and the way in which glass traps it (Schumacher has worked at Norman Foster's office). The acute corner of the Leipzig building suggests that they also enjoy the process of wrapping space in glass. An experimental project made in 1988 in an empty office room in Frankfurt and called 'Sunspots', uses raw light and its kinetic progress through the day as a 'trainer' for their later work in which artificial light is accurately integrated with the controlled nature of the architecture, ceasing to be an adjunct.

These young, successful architects act as a useful model to ambitious students: their own stu-dent work was unconventional; they are clear in their propositions; the spaces are powerful; finesse is a creative adjunct. Needless to say, their lectures about their work are also logical, controlled and wise.

Essay by Peter Cook

Gabrielle Seifert and Gotz Stockmann have collaborated on a number of projects with the artist Otmar Horl under the name 'Formalhaut'. This has been a consistent, rigorous relationship, going much further than the mere gesture of 'involving the artist'. Their development in the 1980s and 1990s has been linked to the simultaneous pursuit of the 'reduced', the 'skin' (reflected in the name, Formalhaut – 'formal skin'), the statemental (an essential in the setting of many of their 'art applied to buildings' competition projects) and, more recently, the creation of a middle-German architecture that is wry and reflective without being coy or Historicist.

Seifert and Stockmann have spent a great deal of time as teachers, as instigators of workshops and as exhibitors. Their well-known view of a field of cows, in which each animal is contained within a translucent plastic 'shed', and the subsequent 'chess game' where the plastic cylinders are overt, full-size quotations of a Seifert/Stockmann Minimal house are instances of a sense of humour that is simultaneously naughty (even, at times, self-deprecating) and yet tough in its elimination of subsidiary elements or decoys. These pieces are certainly challenging to the cultural hang-ups of many observers.

Two developmental projects are worth noting in order to pinpoint Seifert and Stockmann's architectural lineage. The first is the sports hall at Hoechst, designed by Seifert and Zvonko Turkali whilst in the employ of a commercial Frankfurt office. Seifert was persuaded to stay on the scheme for two years beyond the competition stage and the building displays the same statemental quality as the 'art' pieces whilst also being highly competent within the 'hi-tech' language. The other is a competition project for the Frankfurt anthropology museum (largely Stockmann's work), which precedes by a few years the advent of the minimally skinned 'Bloid' or 'Blob' buildings that appeared on many computer screens in the mid 1990s.

The house at Biedenkopf is quite different, for it assembles a carefully poised series of parts. First is the base, which is deceptively calm (on close inspection, one finds that it is modulated). Then the two towers: one, reminiscent of a disused lighthouse, is substantial and tapered; the other is a mere will-o'-the-wisp made of thin woven timbers and plenty of air. In a brooding, near-suburban landscape, the house turns itself towards the mysterious-looking long view and the

fourth main element: a low mound at the end of the field-like garden. The house is almost romantic and certainly quizzical in its assembly of these odd parts, yet it is not whimsical and displays no-nonsense detailing.

Seifert and Stockmann have also investigated building systems; won a competition for a nursery school (in which the 'sustainable technology' aspects of the brief have been responded to with creativity and intelligence whilst avoiding sentimentality); developed a range of 'popular' small house types; and built some steel bridges (together with Martin Heusle and the engineer Claus Bollinger). Their portfolio has yet to include a piece of social housing, an office block or a municipal structure. Indeed, their work is formalistically and intellectually to one side of the German main-stream. Too influenced by the English-speaking world to follow Ungers in the 1980s, too thorough to join the many imitators of Behnisch in the early 1990s and too intelligent to settle on an easy Minimalist formula, they sometimes suffer from this independence and determination, which clearly relates back to their art connections.

Almost as a symbol of this position comes the developed stage of their work on their house in Gelnhausen: a site upon which they have owned the existing residence for many years and which carries childhood memories for both of them. They have finally achieved planning permission for a new house that will almost exactly profile the typical steep-roofed and detached structure of the old one. There the resemblance ends. Many windows are mechanically placed and punched into the 'house' form. The interior is evacuated except for a tray or balcony at high level. Five

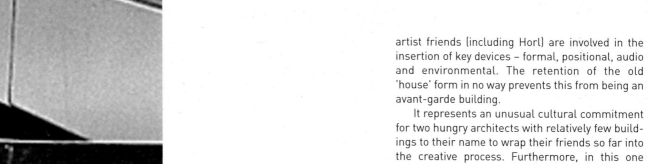

artist friends (including Horl) are involved in the insertion of key devices – formal, positional, audio and environmental. The retention of the old 'house' form in no way prevents this from being an avant-garde building.

It represents an unusual cultural commitment for two hungry architects with relatively few buildings to their name to wrap their friends so far into the creative process. Furthermore, in this one small (and deceptive) building, they seem to be making simultaneous statements about the hermetic state of culture. Preservation in a small European town, they suggest, can be challenged – especially by its own children – exercising their love-hate relationship with it. The strange differences of morality, intensity, motivation that are increasingly emerging at the end of the twentieth century between artists and architects can (occasionally) be faced and resolved.

The Geofluidic Landscape

Sea, Land, Air Assemblage 1997:
model (top) Geofluidic landscape
Multi-layered elevational study (bottom)

A physical, perceptible boundary or edge separates the three elements of sea, land and air. An investigation exploring the notion of this edge condition examines in particular the volatile point at which the interaction and interdependence of each element breaks down. The collapsing edge can be observed for a brief moment before a boundary decays and is subsequently re-established through a cyclical interaction. The boundary becomes blurred as a narrow zone of interference develops. Within this band the true characteristics of the elements are exposed and exaggerated. The edges of interference become edges of influence.

The assemblage formalises the non-tangible characteristics of the three elements and defines edge in relation to their three-dimensional interaction. A dynamic system of three zones – airscape, seascape and landscape are each portrayed in a specific relationship to one another. Kites, pitons and floats are notional characters used to amplify the edges of interference. The characters perform in a continually readjusted spatial relationship.

The airscape is occupied by a flock of kites, which glide and hover above the seascape; this is defined at sea level by a series of horizontal arms that register the fluctuating edge. The landscape is depicted as a layer of fissured rocks through which a network of cords lace the kites' anchoring pitons. Magnetic connections, cams, tilt switches and counterbalances are positioned to sustain a transitory cyclical relationship between the three zones.

Disturbance of the air currents sporadically creates fluctuations in the kites' flight and causes them to plunge momentarily below the sea edge. A break in the edge is detected by tilting arms, which initiate fans to raise the flock. The pitons abrade the rock surface as they are 'dragged' by the conflicting forces of the air and the sea space.

A building proposal for Oslo similarly adopts a strategy that exploits an existing environment of indistinct boundaries. The surrounding rock landscape is sculpted by water channels and fountains and the building is also punctured, invaded and manoeuvred by the dynamic landscape. The building explores in form and programme the natural cycles and processes that are present in the surrounding physical landscape and apparent in the ambient qualities of the peninsula site.

Diurnal light (ranging from natural to artificial), tidal movements, scale, texture and colour are highlighted and accentuated. These are experienced with heightened sensitivity by means of hot pools, viewpoints, sun-drenched platforms, and so forth, concealed within the main functions of the site.

The primary function of the building and its associated elements is to provide a suitable environment for growth. The building can be broadly divided into three parts – two 'gardens' and a central core of service facilities. The first garden produces vegetables and fruits on a horizontal landscape of allotments. These are both natural and controlled areas related to sub-arctic climatic and environmental considerations.

The second garden is an artificial environment consisting of algae tanks for fish food. The algae are suspended in vertical sacks and are propagated by intense artifical light. The 'light box' intentionally spills light to the north, directly back to Oslo, and south, redirected by mirrors, to form modulating stripes of light on the flanks of the building.

A layered painting depicts conceptual and realistic two- and three-dimensional representations of the landscape elevation. The first layer is considered with reference to specific narratives of the scheme and their extrapolated time paths. Light is shown emanating from fissures in the peripheral buildings and highlighting the facade. Light is also depicted projecting away from the peninsula site. Transitory lift boxes, travelling vertically through the building, are shown in multiple positions, as are the service trolleys, which move swiftly around the landscape. The dots and dashes journey at a varying pace and diagrammatically suggest the level and specifics of occupation. The coastal facade is perceived from a greater distance and therefore these visual indicators are at a greater scale and a slower pace.

The second layer also indicates directional light but rationalises the landscape by detailing rock troughs and fluidic switching devices, which power the moving parts of the architecture. Elements such as algae-growing bags, compost hoppers, fountains, jets and fluidic switches are shown in greater detail.

When the front two layers are fully lowered, a 1:200 model of the long section of the building is revealed. The section shows a structural wall and the extruded 'U'-section articulation of bench/trench service areas, the access ramps and raised beds of the allotment, the tilting gardens and jacking bladders exposed on the left. In the main core of the building are the storage lifts and the service areas for vegetable and fish processing, with the kitchen above. To the top right is the breakfast bar, restaurant and kitchen.

The landscape on mass is analogous to the pattern and workings of a microscopic Integrated Circuit etched on to silicon. But unlike the Integrated Circuit ·the landscape computer, with its processors and decision-making, is observable, the electricity being replaced with flows of water and its inputs, gates and outputs becoming fountains, small pools and jets. These corresponding visual indicators illustrate the intricacies of the dynamic system. The complex choreography of the landscape, building and fluidic devices perform in a reciprocal, though never repetitive, sequence.

# Lebbeus woods

Essay by Neil Spiller

Wheel house

The geometry of relationships between light, energy, and matter informs the structure of each and is manifest throughout the physical world. For the term geometry, meaning 'earth measure-ment', I have substituted the more universal term metricality, understood simply as 'measure'. Metricality is the underlying structure of the measurable fabric woven by light in space and time; the order of universal light-metrical fabric has been pre-cisely developed in general relativity theory, quantum field theory, and quantum mechanics. The various metrical systems employed by these theoretical constructs are most often geometrical in kind and have superseded purely algebraic expressions of physical continuity through all scales of the physical world, from the nuc-lear to the cosmic. At the human scale, which is my sole concern here, light, energy, matter and their fundamental equivalence are profoundly comprehended in architectonic form.
Lebbeus Woods ONEFIVEFOUR Princeton Architectural Press (New York) 1989 p.1

Lebbeus Woods first burst on to the London architectural scene in February 1984 when he gave a lecture at the Architectural Association, followed by an exhibition. Coming across this exhibition, the full force of his work hit me in the face. A jaded postgraduate architectural student, I was inspired by the power of his work, its visionary, enigmatic cities and buildings. Woods was concerned with the weird, outrageous dyna-mics and geometries of the quantum and cosmic zone. He brought these ideas together in unlikely urban scenarios for the inhabitants of an almost parallel universe, perhaps that of our architectural future, or an opportunity we have already lost. He seemed to me a late-twentieth-century Piranesi.

Since his early projects, Woods has been less concerned with the peculiar anomalies of space-time and has carried his preoccupations into the war zone. His work has engaged with the politics of forming space in areas that have felt the full force of political expediency and bloody domestic unheaval. He has just produced the book RADICAL RECONSTRUCTION (Princeton), which seeks to explore the complex rela-tionships between war, architecture and reconstruction. His interest in the human subject and condition far exceeds the normative meanderings of traditional architectural practice. Humanity, its liberation, its catastrophes (both natural and unnatural) and its freedom, is cen-tral to all his recent work. His is an architecture against 'zero tolerance', about the mitigation of pain, strife and political and aesthetic bondage. Even more remarkably, Woods has the optimism to believe that architecture is of value in this con-text. It is a breath of fresh air set against the foul exhausts of much contemporary architectural production.

RADICAL RECONSTRUCTION is an apt title. It takes us on a journey – some paths are implied, some are explicit – that questions and reformulates archi-tecture's constituent parts. One by one, meaning, function, representation, abstraction et al are run through the mill and recast within the contexts of war and cataclysmic social and physical fracture. The recent projects are set in Sarajevo, Havana and San Francisco, simultaneously mediating between many boundaries. Like Woods' concept of 'free space', his drawings give much elbow room to the reader, a huge amount being left unsaid. The viewer/reader can bring their own preoccu-pations to bear on the images, imagining other worlds and other technologies that may have been used to create such distinct yet fluctuating architectures.

Like the architecture, the drawings are not exclusively pragmatic or poetic. There is oblique space within the work, which fosters personal readings. This is tolerance of another kind: Wood's spaces are 'free', unencumbered by functional naming. He tolerates, but is not ambivalent about, cruelty in politics, in capitalism. He is clear about blind human perseverance and survival. He attempts to ease all these dilemmas but at the

High houses Sarajevo:
reconstruction of the air-space
(opposite and below)

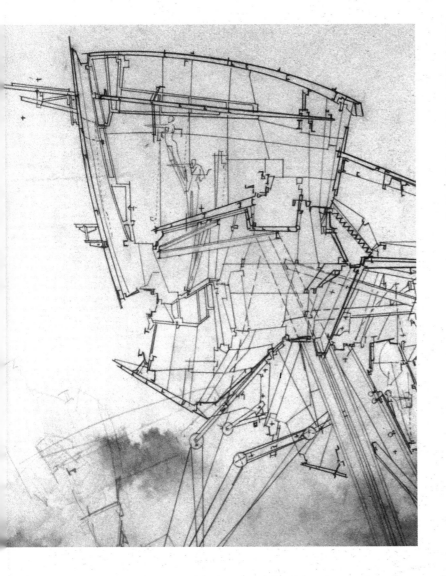

same time to find a creative struggle. As Captain Beefheart has said: 'The way I keep in touch with the world is very gingerly because it touches too hard.' Woods' work is insurance against this hard touch while using creatively some of the hardest touches the world has to give. He refuses to accept normal architecture in all its manifestations. Normal architecture is nothing if not a conspiracy of capitalist vested interests, social manipulation and aesthetic fascism. Woods' work is a critique against the rhetoric of Reductivism and Mini-malism. This is 'full-on' Maximalist architecture. It is an acknowledgement that the practice of architecture exists within a beautiful complexity.

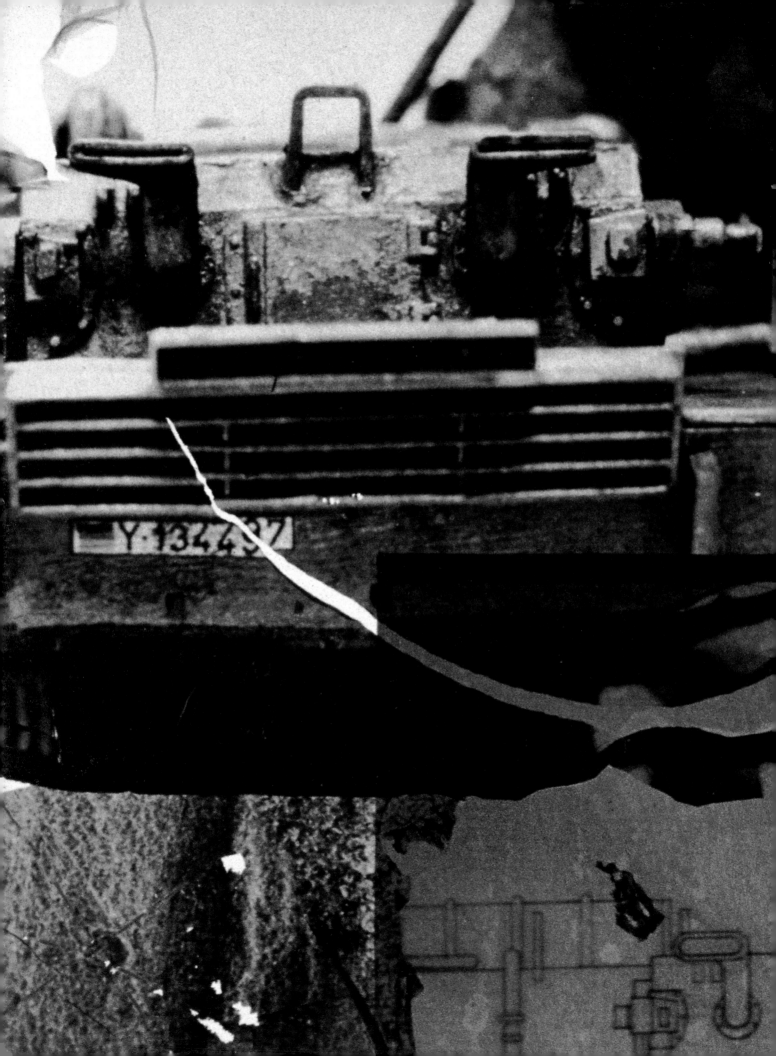

masahiko yendo

## Urban Experience: The Megapolis

Design for mass urban structure

Unlike the metropolis, the megapolis no longer sustains a singular ideology; rather, it is made up of multiple elements and a simultaneous development of autonomous parts, mutating our indigenous selves into a mass urban structure.

In this heterogeneous coexistence, individuals and the collective mass are in a semiotic relationship. The fulfilment of one's desire and the greater interest of the society are one and the same. In the urban cosmopolis the identity of the individual is preserved by the diversity of the ever-expanding multitude. The urban reality mobilises the tactile, the incidental, the transitory, the expendable and the intuitive knowledge. It does not involve abstract aesthetic research amongst privileged objects of attention, but a mobile order of sense, taste and desire. In the rapid and perpetual consumption of information and products, the only constant is inevitable change and transformation. Nothing and no one can withstand the destructive nature of the change, yet it will liberate and expand the consciousness, creating new order, entity and environment. Our striving for perfection has equated to striving for ultimate stability, yet the sheer size of the entity fosters the development of new identities within the whole. Uncertainty represents anxiety, chaos and lack of stability. Stability in turn symbolises comfort, predictability and certainty. Complete stability, however, will be inflexible, oppressive and forever close to being dead. By the laws of physics, the entity tends towards stability, but on the other hand, by the simple laws of probability, movement on the whole tends towards greater diversity. This is the irony of existence. This is the essence of the city.

### The City

There is a moment of silence when every object is grey and projects a greyness, before the arrival of dawn; no presence of light or shadow, a void of time and space, a place that evolves, decays, which liberates us, and represses us.

Glowing on the dark horizon, like an insect attracted towards light, the blinding torch of a city. Pixels of light become windows. The vertical fortress pulls us towards its pulse. A thumping metropolis whose tower-like tentacles spit steam into the sky. A labyrinth of steel meshed together like roots of a tree. A back alley constructed from refuse. Street lights reveal wretched left-over spaces. Clusters of deteriorated steel boxes, assembled from industrial parts. Mechanical elements bulge from decayed structures. Naked pipes wrap around each other in bondage. Loose wires, rusted steel panels, chipped paint, layered walls encapsulate the essence of the city.

This sinful place does not creep into hiding. It exists. It is emotional, temperamental, irrational, lacks continuity, and is as logical as we are. It embodies memories, ongoing events and future anticipation. A manifestation of our lives, ideas and knowledge. Trapped by limitations, furthered by possibilities. In its destruction, and construction, its form, and shadow, in its pavement and its walls, it changes, and evolves. In its density and complexity we cannot help but find ourselves.

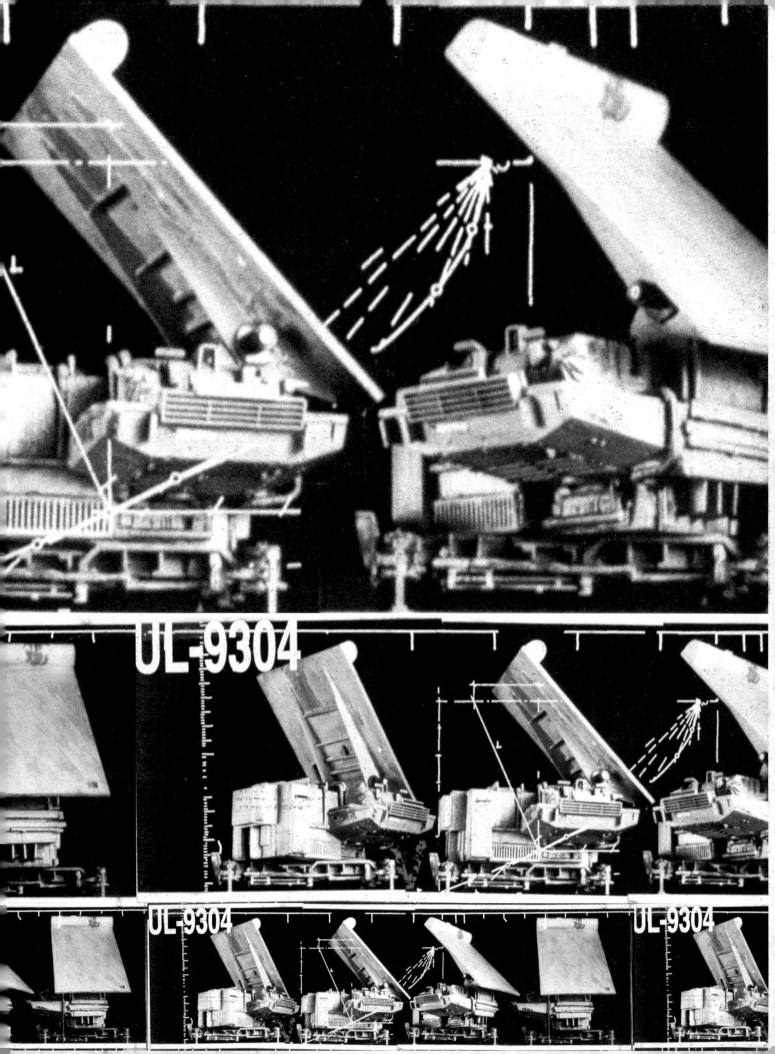

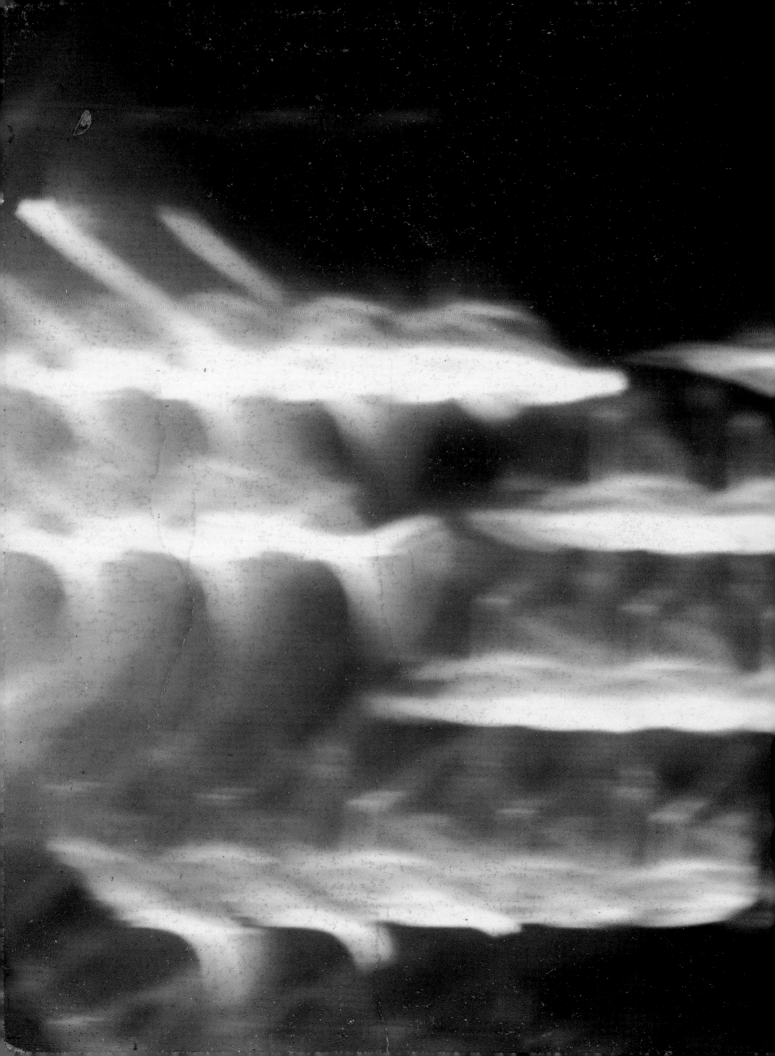